TEACHING READING
TO STUDENTS WITH
LIMITED ENGLISH PROFICIENCIES

TEACHING READING
TO STUDENTS WITH
LIMITED ENGLISH PROFICIENCIES

By

BETTY ANDERSON, Ed.D.

From the University of Maryland
Professor, University of Central Florida
Orlando, Florida

and

ROSIE WEBB JOELS, Ph.D.

From the University of Arizona
Associate Professor, University of Central Florida
Orlando, Florida

CHARLES C THOMAS • PUBLISHER
Springfield • Illinois • U.S.A.

Published and Distributed Throughout the World by
CHARLES C THOMAS • PUBLISHER
2600 South First Street
Springfield, Illinois 62717

© *1986 by* CHARLES C THOMAS • PUBLISHER
ISBN 0-398-05179-8
Library of Congress Catalog Card Number: 85-17125

With **THOMAS BOOKS** *careful attention is given to all details of manufacturing
and design. It is the Publisher's desire to present books that are satisfactory as to their
physical qualities and artistic possibilities and appropriate for their particular use.*
THOMAS BOOKS *will be true to those laws of quality that assure a good name
and good will.*

Printed in the United States of America
Q-R-3

Library of Congress Cataloging in Publication Data

Anderson, Betty, 1982-
   Teaching reading to students with limited English
proficiencies.

   Bibliography: p.
   Includes index.
   1. English language--Study and teaching--Foreign
speakers. 2. Reading. I. Joels, Rosie Webb. II. Title.
PE1128.A2A535   1985   428.4'07   85-17125
ISBN 0-398-05179-8

PREFACE

CLASSROOM TEACHERS are likely to have children in their classrooms today who have limited proficiency in English. Those whose native language is Spanish are by far the largest group, but children who speak languages from French to Farsi are increasingly likely to appear in classrooms throughout the United States. To a monolingual classroom teacher, simple communication with such pupils is a daily challenge and reading instruction may appear to be an impossible task. *Teaching Reading to Students with Limited English Proficiencies* (LEP) is offered as a resource for teachers responsible for teaching reading to pupils whose native language is not English. It may be especially valuable for those with only an isolated LEP student or those without the assistance of a bilingual program.

In Chapter One, an historical overview of past and current philosophies of education for limited English speakers is traced. From the melting pot to the Bilingual Education Act, the background of changing outlooks for educators is briefly reviewed.

Current programs are described in Chapter Two. Various interpretations at state and local levels of legislative requirements are discussed. The likely effects for classroom teachers for each type of program, particularly for reading instruction, are also presented. Regardless of the type program followed in any state or district, certain underlying principles should guide the teacher who provides reading instruction for LEP students. These are also presented in Chapter Two along with a rationale for their inclusion and their impact upon classroom reading instruction.

Chapter Three is a guide to the features of language that in-

v

fluence a child's achievement in reading. Background information that can help the teacher plan instruction is included.

Several methods and approaches for reading instruction for the LEP student are discussed in Chapter Four. Adaptations in the language experience approach, sight method, basal readers, oral reading methods, and approaches for older learners are suggested. In addition, adaptations for the use of skills management systems with LEP students is included.

Chapter Five presents specific teaching activities for immediate classroom use. Teachers can find ideas here suitable for LEP pupils to help them develop sight vocabulary and word attack skills as well as increasing vocabulary and comprehension of print materials. Modifications of common teaching practices that are appropriate for use with students who are non-native speakers of English are also suggested.

Some of the major points stressed in the earlier chapters are briefly summarized in Chapter Six. Teachers who are challenged by the LEP child in the classroom where English is the medium of instruction will find a wealth of background information and instructional activities in *Teaching Reading to Students with Limited English Proficiencies*. This book serves as a starting point for the teacher's own understanding as classroom practices are adapted in order to guide and assist the LEP student toward improved achievement.

CONTENTS

TEACHING READING
TO STUDENTS WITH
LIMITED ENGLISH PROFICIENCIES

CHAPTER 1

HISTORICAL OVERVIEW

AMERICA has offered her populace educational opportunities on a scale matched by few nations in history. 1983-84 school year student enrollment in elementary and secondary schools exceeded 44 million; a higher percentage of these students will graduate from high school than in any other country (FIP-NEA Advocate, p. 3). These 44 million students represent diverse ethnic and linguistic groups. Among these groups there has been a tradition of inequity to benefit from educational opportunities. This tradition goes back to the nation's birth; Brown v. Topeka in 1954 notwithstanding, equal educational opportunities remain a goal rather than a reality.

Social and political forces within the country's school districts have affected practices resulting in unequal opportunities. For example, citizens' perceived purposes of public schooling have shaped educational policies. These purposes were, and continue to be, as unique as the communities in which they originate; they are more uniform today, however, than they were in earlier times. Though the goals of education differ with geographic diversity, one can find similarities across regions as education's purposes have evolved throughout America's history.

The purposes of education have changed gradually and, at times, with great subtlety. Direction by local leaders generally created an atmosphere of self-management in which change occurred slowly and with few disruptive ancillary movements. Directions of educational goal-setting by authorities removed from the local communities, however, have resulted in changes that occasionally have been counter to local goals. These goals, along with their resulting policies and practices, in some instances have been met with resistance; furthermore, local schools have been disrupted by confliction philosophies and goals.

Changes in purpose, inequality of opportunities, and control of educational policies are related; each is related also to the school experiences of students who have special needs. Students who differ most markedly have often been denied the opportunity to enter school or to achieve at the level of their peers. For example, high achievement (and even access to public schooling) has been denied to those students who lack proficiency in the language of instruction, most frequently English. A brief overview of the history of education in the United States for limited-English-proficiency students provides an historical framework for the remainder of this monograph.

During the 18th and 19th centuries, the purposes of education were chiefly to instill religious beliefs and, related to this, to develop strong moral qualities within the student. Policies were set by local authorities — individuals often active as the leadership of the communities' churches. Schooling was available primarily for those students who were from middle- and upper-class families. There were communities of non-English speaking citizens scattered across the growing nation. Education in these communities differed in character and purpose; most frequently, however, instruction was in the vernacular, the language of the homes, and English, if used at all, was taught as a subject.

Prior to the 1880s, there were many public schools where students experienced learning through a language other than English: German in Central Texas; French in Louisiana; and Spanish in New Mexico (Andersson and Boyer, 1970). The language of each home, of the community, and of the school was usually the same in communities with a high concentration of immigrant families. These families generally shared a common country of origin and shared, therefore, a common language.

The late 19th century brought with it a new wave of immigrants who generally did not speak English and who did not establish communities. Living in large urban areas or scattered in rural areas across the country, students of these families increasingly presented a challenge for public school systems. The challenge for the student was even greater, often insurmountable. Many students, discouraged and unsuccessful, received little or no formal education.

Educational goals changed; schools were viewed as a vehicle for establishing the melting pot in society. This purpose, the blending of cultural and language differences, persisted into the 20th century as immigration, especially from Western Europe, continued. Additionally, a new purpose, promotion of intelligent citizenship, originated in the mid-19th Century and increasingly influenced education policy (Robinson, 1977). This purpose was at its strongest during and following World War I. At that time, the use of a language other than English was grounds for suspicion; those who did not speak English were seen as disloyal by their neighbors.

Many immigrants were anxious to enter the economic mainstream of American life. They hoped also that their children would achieve, both economically and socially. These children did, in fact, enroll in school, acquire skills in English, and achieve at higher academic levels. But, advancements were not uniform, and levels of success were related to language strengths in English.

Many children of foreign-born parents were embarrassed by their parents' "old ways." They were willing to disassociate themselves from their parents' native country culture. One of the most obvious symbols of the parents' origins was their use of a language other than English. The children, therefore, compliantly accepted the dominant language of the community, English, while the schools benignly encouraged abandonment of the non-English mother tongue by immigrant children. In later life, many of these individuals would never speak or hear the language with which they had developed all of their pre-school knowledge; they would no longer be able to communicate in the language with which they had formed bonds with the most significant others in their early lives.

Recent Changes

During the 1950s and 1960s equality of educational opportunities became an articulated priority as federal authorities exercised increased control over America's public schools. The purposes of education came to include maintenance of ethnic and racial heritage; concurrently, there was a growing group identity within ethnic, racial, and linguistic minorities. These groups rejected the melting pot theory and sought to promote cultural pluralism in American society. Culture and language were valued as contributors to society's richness, this composite of differences.

The massive school failure of non-English-speaking children was well documented. Influenced by these data, the United States Congress legislated reforms that would provide equal opportunity for limited-English-proficient (LEP) students (Paulston, 1978). Legislative reforms that would form the basis and funding for bilingual education were Title VI of the Civil Rights Act of 1964 and the Title VII amendment to the 1965 Elementary and Secondary Education Act.

Lau v. Nichols, a Supreme Court decision of 1974, held that equal treatment was not equal opportunity if a student did not speak the language of instruction. This judicial edict, along with legislative mandates and federal regulations, has provided guidance for school districts as programmatic changes were undertaken. Instruction in the mother tongue was the vehicle for meeting the needs of LEP students in many school districts.

President Jimmy Carter issued guidelines in August of 1980, directing that school districts, in complying with federal regulations, must offer instruction in the vernacular, the students' home languages; perhaps having sensed a change in the political direction of the electorate, the United States Congress did not ratify these guidelines. In 1981, the newly-elected President, Ronald Reagan, announced that school districts would have more flexibility in meeting the needs of LEP students. This action was compatible with Reagan's goal of reducing federal interference in local issues.

Instruction in the mother tongue continued in school districts in which it was politically popular; in other locales, alternatives have been utilized. It is instructive to note that many questions remain about the effectiveness of bilingual education programs. In spite of the fact that there has been over a decade of federally-funded programs using a variety of diverse practices, there are few undisputed empirical data related to what constitutes effective methods, competent personnel, or desirable organization in the implementation of bilingual education.

There was, in fact, a seminar in December, 1982, at which investigators reviewed their work in progress. At issue were questions dealing with characteristics of bilingual programs, qualifications of teachers in bilingual programs, effectiveness of differing programs using instruction in the vernacular, and the relationship between language and cognitive skills. Other topics were also discussed, but the need for the seminar was partially based on "the complex nature of the findings" (*Forum*, 1983, p. 2). Thus, it appears that many of the problems are yet to be solved. For example, Carrillo (1977) had described teacher education as a weak component in the system of bilingual programs; it remains so today.

Increased local control of public schools will be accompanied by a diversity of purposes and programs. Children's needs will present renewed challenges for the classroom teachers as students are mainstreamed into educational settings with their age peers. While districts continue to differ in educational philosophy and goals, it is hoped that cultural and language diversity will be valued.

CHAPTER 2

PRACTICAL CONSIDERATIONS

BILINGUAL EDUCATION has been identified as an educational program designed to allow a student to learn academic content in the mother tongue (that is, first language or home language) which is different from the usual language of instruction within a particular school setting. The Bilingual Education Act defined bilingual education as "the use of two languages, one of which is English, as mediums of instruction" (Saville and Troike, 1971). There have evolved, however, a variety of programs which are based on differing definitions, philosophies, and goals.

In some legislation (as in Colorado, for example), bilingualism is joined with biculturalism as programmatic foundations. Study of the history and culture associated with a student's mother tongue is considered to be a vital component of such a bilingual program. Other states, however, have enacted legislation which expressly prohibits the bicultural component (as in Arizona) or does not deal with it. Furthermore, enabling legislation for bilingual education programs has not been necessarily enacted in or limited to those states with high percentages of students with a home language other than English. While California has a state law supporting bilingual programs, as does Massachusetts, Florida does not.

Programs

Bilingual programs have differed in their goals as well as definitions. Goals have been reflected in two basic program types, that is, maintenance and transition. Maintenance programs have, as one

9

goal, maintaining (even improving) language skills in the first language while the student acquires a second language. Transition programs, on the other hand, utilize the home language as the medium of instruction only until the second language is learned. Thus, there is a transition to the second language as the medium of instruction with no further utilization of or instruction in the first language.

There are many variations of these program types and, in some cases, programs that combine characteristics of each. Programmatic variety is related to the ties between program types and eductional goals of a community. If, for example, one valued cultural pluralism and hoped to promote it in communities with large numbers of students who entered school speaking a language other than English, one would develop a program primarily maintenance in nature. An extension of this program type would be one in which biliteracy is the goal for both majority language speakers and minority language speakers (Cohen, 1976). A transition program, however, would be appropriate if one's goal is to enable students to become users of the community's dominant language both in the school setting and in the broader context of the social and economic life of the community and the nation.

MacKay, Barkman, and Jordan (1979) have edited a collection of works in which the teacher of LEP students can find valuable insights. While including theoretical writings, the chapters also cover practices in second language reading. The writers, throughout the book, view reading as an active, meaningful process.

Guiding Principles

The patchwork of existing programs has been criticized as not being based on social or pedagogical rationale. As pointed out earlier, local and state agencies have failed to reach an agreement on the long-term goals of educating LEP students or the methods by which the goals will be reached. Resistance to federal guidelines has been based on a variety of issues: proportion of LEP students in the community, tenured teachers monolingual in the majority language, lack of trained personnel fluent in LEP students' language, and the cost of additional programs.

There are approximately 3.5 million students in the United States who speak little or no English. Those enrolled in transitional bilingual education utilize their mother tongue as the medium of instruction only until they have mastered English to such an extent that they can function in the English language within the school setting. Others may be in maintenance programs which utilize the home language as an initial tool for instruction and continue to enhance oral language fluency (even literacy) in that language while developing skills in English. There are many additional LEP students who find themselves in programs where the only problem confronted is their lack of English skills. Frequently, instruction in English as a second language (ESL) is carried out by a volunteer or paraprofessional who may or may not be fluent in the student's language and who may lack professional training in education. These instructors do not often deal with achievement in other areas and their students must cope as best they can during instruction in other curricular subjects in their regular classrooms.

Both bilingual education and ESL programs present the regular classroom teacher with a challenge when those programs require the pulling out of LEP students from the regular classroom for a scheduled daily lesson. The fact remains that many teachers are monolingual in English and LEP students spend all or much of the school day with these teachers. The degree of success the teacher and the students attain in the classroom depends on many factors, many of which are interrelated.

It is beyond the teacher's ability to deal with some of the factors that have been identified as related to school achievement. For example, past educational experiences, for good or ill, are over. In addition, the language spoken in the home is an established fact, as is the socio-economic level of the family. This is not to say that the teacher cannot influence students' scholastic progress, but it is constructive to keep in mind that a teacher's effectiveness is more strongly influenced by flexibility, interpersonal perspectives, teaching competencies, and resourcefulness within all subject areas.

The teacher's flexibility and resourcefulness in reading instruction are especially crucial for the LEP student who is in a regular classroom. If English is the language of instruction, the student who lacks proficiency in English needs some definite and continuing considerations. The student has special needs in all the curricular subjects; these needs are especially acute in reading and will best be met by the teacher who is willing to develop the knowledge, skills, and attitude appropriate for helping the LEP student.

Knowledge includes an understanding of the child, the child's language and culture, and areas of probable mismatch between the child's language and culture and those of the school and community. Teaching competencies appropriate for working with LEP students do not differ in kind as much as they differ in degree. That is, effective teaching behaviors should be applied during instruction with the LEP child to an even greater degree. Some of the behaviors related to teacher effectiveness include: thorough planning for instructional goals, communication clarity, purpose setting, prompt and frequent feedback, and diagnostic and prescriptive teaching.

Attitudes and enhancement of the affective climate are important for all learners. For the LEP student, however, there is an even greater need to build a positive, supportive environment. The teacher needs to exhibit a feeling that the student has worth as an individual and as a member of the class. Nonacceptance of the child's language within the classroom brings with it the danger that the child will develop feelings which are destructive to achievement. Thonis (1970), after describing specific teaching activities throughout *Teaching Reading to NonEnglish Speakers*, concludes this book with purposes of the proposed program. Prominent among the purposes are enhancement of students' self-esteem, provision for sense of pride, and prevention of pupils' alienation. Teacher qualities which would create a positive climate include an understanding and friendly personality, confidence, and genuine respect for all students.

Assumptions

The stated need for the teacher to acquire appropriate knowledge, competencies, and attitudes is based on some assumptions underlying effective reading instruction for the LEP child. These assumptions are the following: the reading process is language dependent, reading achievement is preceded by prior concept development, and learning is best promoted by positive development of affective factors.

Language dependency. As one of the four language arts, reading is greatly related to the child's strengths and weaknesses in listening, speaking and writing. Ching (1976) states that listening and speaking abilities in English are essential for success in reading. Reading strategies used to unlock unknown words and phrases are first learned as oralaural skills to express and receive thoughts. A child, for example, who has not acquired the ability to distinguish likenesses and differences among significant speech sounds in a particular language will not be able to use phonics as a decoding aid to read in that language. The child who cannot utilize tacit knowledge of word order (that is, grammatical rules for structuring meaningful expressions) will be unable to use syntax as a type of context clue. Examples of these and other specific language differences will be described in a subsequent section.

Concept development. The act of reading involves the reconstruction of meaning expressed by the writer. The reader and the writer must share some common experiences or background knowledge in order for the reader to accurately comprehend the text. The lack of earlier experiences related to curricular topics or themes contributes to low reading achievement; a word, even though accurately pronounced, is a nonsense word to a child who brings no meaning to that word or to most of the surrounding words in the text. Relating this to assumption number one, language dependency of the reading process, meaningful words have earlier become part of the child's speaking and listening vocabularies. Children learn to enrich both their language and informational background by many exposures to experiences in their world and to words that describe that world.

Affective factors. These factors are, perhaps, the most important influences on reading achievement. Interest, motivation, self-concept, and attitude are receiving less and less attention as school districts utilize management systems and emphasize isolated skills. Yet, children need to feel secure and acquire some measure of success in all learning activities in order to maintain a high level of interest. In classrooms, one can see positive evidence of these factors when a child pays attention, is enthusiastic, and is actively participating. Children feel the sensitivity and caring of teachers, and they will be more successful when treated with respect and taught through methods based on an awareness of their special needs.

CHAPTER 3

LANGUAGE DIFFERENCES

W HEN TEACHERS are assigned to teach reading to a lin-
guistically different child, their success depends greatly on
an understanding of the child's language. Specifically, the teacher
should be aware of the contrasts that occur in the components of
English and those of the child's mother tongue. These language
components include phonology, syntax, and sematics. Phonology is
the inventory of meaningful speech sounds used in a specific language, syntax is the word ordering rules used to form grammatical
structures in a language, and semantics refers to the meaning of a
word or group of words.

An understanding of linguistic contrasts, whether they be in
phonology, syntax, or semantics will enable the teacher to develop
teaching strategies which accentuate the abilities of the limited English proficiency (LEP) child. Additionally, this understanding will
facilitate instructional practices which avoid emphasizing those
reading skills most likely to cause confusion and present undue difficulties for the student. In reading instruction, a progam's primary
focus should be upon developing meaning through comprehension
abilities. Conversely, stress on smaller linguistic units, for example,
phonemes and syllables should be minimized.

Phonology

Phonemes are the smallest speech sounds which can change
meaning; they are without meaning of their own. For illustration,
an examination of the contrastive phonological features of English

15

and Spanish will be described in this discussion. Nilsen and Nilsen (1973), however, present a more thorough analysis of phonological differences not only between Spanish and English, but between English and 49 other languages. Nilsen and Nilsen serves as a very valuable reference for the teacher of an LEP student, as does Saville and Troike (1971), if the student's mother tongue is Spanish or Navaho.

Saville and Troike depict predictable problem areas by comparing the phonemes of Spanish and English. Their data on consonant phonemes were adapted for Table 1.

An examination of Table 1 reveals that there are 14 instances of agreement when the 24 English consonant phonemes are compared with the 18 Spanish phonemes. The ten English consonant phonemes that do not occur in Spanish will be confused with other phonemes that are similar in articulation. It is important to reiterate that phonemes are the smallest sound unit which can change meaning. Thus, if phonemic differentiations are not perceived by a listener, similar words may be homonyms for that listener.

While consonant phonemes may cause confusion for the LEP child, the greatest areas of difficulty exists among vowel phonemes when the two languages are Spanish and English. From data in Saville and Troike (1971), Table 2 was developed to contrast the vowel phonemes of Spanish with those of English.

These tables reveal the areas of possible mismatch for a child who has Spanish as a first language and who attempts to identify English phonemes. Such a child will have developed a phonological system based on the phonemes of Spanish, and the child will attempt to fit into this system the phonemes of English. A Spanish phoneme category, for example, may be used to accommodate similar, but separate, English phonemes, and may result in the listener auditorially perceiving as identical the two English words which differ only in the specific phonemes. Examples of these phonemic differentiations (or lack of them) are shown in Table 3 (Saville and Troike, 1971).

The first example in Table 3 is the /č/ phoneme category. In Spanish, it may be pronounced /č/ as in *chore* or /š/ as in *shore*. The

Table 1

CONSONANT: PHONEMES

Shared in English and Spanish:

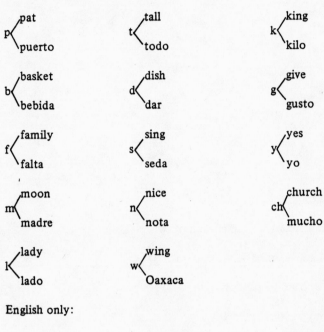

p — pat / puerto
t — tall / todo
k — king / kilo

b — basket / bebida
d — dish / dar
g — give / gusto

f — family / falta
s — sing / seda
y — yes / yo

m — moon / madre
n — nice / nota
ch — church / mucho

l — lady / lado
w — wing / Oaxaca

English only:

sh - shop	t͟h - then	ng - sing
j - jam	ž - azure	z - zip
th - thin	h - hope	r - run
v - van		

Spanish only:

ř - rancho (single trill)	x - examen	ñ - mañana
r̃ - perro (multiple trill)		

Table 2

VOWEL PHONEMES

English:

ē - b<u>ee</u>t	ă - bat	ī - <u>i</u>ce
ĭ - b<u>i</u>t	ŭ - b<u>u</u>t	ŏ - b<u>o</u>x
ā - b<u>ai</u>t	ō - b<u>oa</u>t	ô - f<u>ou</u>ght
ĕ - b<u>e</u>t	â - ch<u>air</u>	ōō - r<u>u</u>le
ŏŏ - l<u>oo</u>k	oi - <u>oi</u>l	ou - <u>ou</u>t
ä - h<u>o</u>bby		

Spanish:

i - m<u>i</u> (similiar to i in mach<u>i</u>ne)

a - m<u>a</u>sa (similiar to musical note f<u>a</u>)

e - d<u>e</u> (similiar to musical note r<u>e</u>)

o - c<u>o</u>mo (similiar to g<u>o</u>)

u - g<u>u</u>sto (similiar to <u>u</u>kelele)

Table 3

PHONEMIC DIFFERENTIATIONS

Spanish		English
ch		chop
		shop
s		sip
		zip
n		win
		wing
b		ban
		van
t		tin
		thin
s		sin
d		den
		then
y		yet
		jet
i		cheap
		chip
e		bait
		bet
		bat
a		cut
		cot
u		Luke
		look
o		coat
		caught

Reference: Saville and Troike

pronunciation differences in Spanish, however, never signal a change in meaning. The Spanish-first-language (SL1) student may not hear as different minimally contrastive pairs of English words using the /č/ and /š/ phonemes. Examples of these word pairs include *cheap-sheep, chop-shop, match-mash, witch-wish,* and *catching-cashing,* all of which could be homonyms for the SL1 student.

Compounding this area of confusion is the fact that some phonemes in Spanish may not occur in a particular position (initial, medial, or final) or within a specific phoneme context. The initial phoneme of *Durango* is not difficult to pronounce when encountered in the word *Dan.* Between vowels, however, the letter d in a Spanish word represents a phoneme similar to the beginning phoneme of the English word *this.* Thus, the child may not perceive as different the English words *ladder* and *lather.*

The category of English voiced consonant phonemes does not exist in Spanish. These phonemes are underlined in the following words: *j*et, *v*an, *th*en, and *z*oo. These words may be perceived as the following words: *y*et, *b*an, *d*en, and *s*ue, respectively.

There are also consonant blends that never occur in Spanish and which are predictable areas of confusion for the SL1 reader. Examples include beginning *s* blends. Similar words may exist in Spanish but the *s* is preceded by the letter *e,* creating a separate syllable. Instances of some *s* blend words and their Spanish counterparts are: *s*chool, *e*scuela; *s*pecial, *e*special; and *s*tation, *e*stación.

It is hoped that the preceding discussion will provide some insights into some of the complex contrasts between the phonological systems of Spanish and English. Similar areas of confusion are likely to occur between other languages and English. In light of these, it is hoped that teachers will be dissuaded from developing a reading program that stresses phonics skills at the expense of more meaningful competencies, such as using contextual analysis and acquiring comprehension.

Syntax

Another component of langauge is syntax, the word ordering rules for forming grammatical expressions. Again using Spanish as an example, predictable problems can be identified for the LEP student who has internalized the syntactic rules of Spanish. These problems involve the student's anticipating "what comes next" in terms of word order. By correctly hypothesizing that a noun will follow an adjective, for example, the student can reduce the possibilities for an unknown word. If Spanish syntax is imposed on an English text, however, errors and confusion result.

Adjectives. In English, the noun would follow the adjective, as in: The *mean* dog. The Spanish construction would be: El perro *bajo*. Especially perplexing are descriptor series, as found in: The old gray black man; or, The big green luxury car. The word order would be different in Spanish; and if the order of the descriptors is changed to fit Spanish syntax, the expression in English sounds awkward and perhaps loses its intended meaning.

Contractions. Spanish has only two contracted forms, *al* (from a el) and *del* (from de el). English has many contractions, and perhaps most confusing are those that have a change in vowel sound of the verb. If the SL1 has acquired in his listening vocabulary the words *is* and *not*, it is a less difficult task to progress to *isn't* than it is to progress from listening vocabulary words of *will* and *not* to *won't*.

Possessive. Spanish syntax requires the use of the word *de* (*of*, in English) preceding the possessor. *El libro de Maria* would be translated to: *Maria's book*. Confusion may result for the SL1 student who is accustomed to hearing the *s* as a signal for plural. The phrase, *the book's pages*, will convey inaccurate meaning if the reader fails to comprehend that the expression is describing multiple pages of one book.

Articles. The Spanish articles *el, la, los,* and *las* indicate the gender and number (singular and plural) of the noun following. Each of these articles would be replaced by the English *the*. Further difficulties arise when the child uses the pronouns *he, she, him,* and *her* rather than *it* to refer to inanimate objects which, in Spanish, would be either masculine or femine. An additional area of confusion results from the fact that articles are frequently omitted in some Spanish expressions. For example, *El es doctor* would be literally translated to *He is doctor* and is an expected construction within the oral language of the child who has dominant language skills in Spanish.

Negation. Spanish always requires a negative before the verb while English does not. The Spanish expression *No tengo nada* would be translated literally to the English *I do not have nothing*. The double negative constuction is acceptable in Spanish and is frequently used by the SL1 student who is acquiring English oral language skills.

Idiomatic phrases. Many phrases in Spanish must be translated as thought units in order to convey meaning. *Tengo sed* literally is translated to *I have thirst*. The expressions for age and hunger are similarly constructed. *Good morning* is translated *Buenos días* (literally, good days). These expressions in English, as well as English figurative language phrases, are examples of langauge expressions that should be taught as wholes and should always be presented in meaningful context. For example, the meaning of the whole phrase *it was raining cats and dogs* is not the sum of its individual parts. A child who attempts to discern the phrase's meaning by putting together the meanings of the individual words will be confused and inaccurate. While these examples were related to Spanish, similar confusions occur for speakers of other languages.

Semantics

The final area of this language difference description deals with meaning and vocabulary. Especially troublesome, as noted previously, are the idiomatic expressions that exist in both languages. It is suggested that during instruction meaningful context always surround these expressions that should be taught as whole units. Also, as described earlier, the influence of phonology will result in many different word pairs in English being perceived as homonyms and conveying inaccurate meanings.

Frequently, there is no exact word for a particular word in the other language. Or there may be one word for more than one concept or for multiple words in the other language. In Spanish, specifically, the word *en* depends on context for its translation. It may be: *at home* for *en casa*; *upon the table* for *en la mesa*; or *on the wall* for *en la pared*.

Conclusions

Speakers of a language have acquired systems for differentiating speech sounds, for ordering words into grammatical expressions, and for assigning meaning to words. These systems are specific to each language and, therefore, differ across langauges. Some languages are closely related, for example, Spanish and Portugese, and their systems are more alike than those systems of very different languages, such as, English and Vietnamese.

A student who is learning to read in a language in which he has limited listening and speaking abilities will be faced with many challenges. Varied approaches have been utilized with LEP students and have been found to have advantages and disadvantages. Vernacular instruction (teaching in the child's first language) has been utilized in some schools, especially those with a high proportion of LEP students sharing a common native langauge. English as a second language has been another approach, but the emphasis in this approach is on teaching English skills rather than on progress in the curriculum areas.

Many classroom teachers are responsible for the school achievement of one or more LEP students for whom little or no auxiliary services are provided. For these teachers, it may not be a question of which special program to put the child in, which langauge to use, or even which approach to use. The most realistic expectation is for the teacher to adapt the approaches she is currently using, whether they are basal reader, language experience, or individualized reading approaches, and to utilize specific abilities which are most easily developed for the child at that time.

The knowledge and sensitivity of the classroom teacher will direct the ways in which reading instruction is facilitated for the LEP student, and specific suggestions for approaches and teaching strategies will be discussed in later sections of this work. It should be noted, however, that these suggestions are only a small start toward maximizing achievement opportunities for the child. Understanding the languages' differences will provide a foundation and rationale for subsequent instructional planning. Pragmatism should guide further planning; if, after a reasonable time, a specific teaching strategy is not productive, another strategy should be tried.

The evaluation of a strategy's usefulness should focus on the desired outcome of reading instruction. Keeping in mind that the act of reading involves bringing meaning to and getting meaning from text, it will be unproductive (and frustrating) to stress phonics or nonsense words. Strategies which stress comprehension are strongly recommended. The word attack skill most helpful in stressing meaning is contextual analysis. Contextual analysis should always be one of a combination of strategies used to unlock unknown words.

The need to emphasize contextual analysis and comprehension is important for all students, but it is especially strong for the LEP student. Reading requires the student to break a code (to decipher marks on the page) in order to reach the meaningful thoughts expressed by the code. The code, the smaller units from words, to syllables, to letters and sounds, carry progressively less meaning. If these smaller units are emphasized, especially out of context, there is the danger that a child will view reading's goal as merely sounding out words. Most teachers are familiar with this type of reader; the prolific word caller, the child who reads aloud with accuracy and expression, yet comprehends little of a text's message.

The reasons for stressing comprehension for the LEP student include an additional, and stronger, factor. The LEP student has many differences between his code and that of a text written in English. The components of language (phonics, syntax, and word meanings), as previously discussed, have many areas of difference, and it is through these components that the code is structured. The student has, however, fewer differences in underlying thought units, concepts, or ideas. Depending on the experiential background of the child, many prior understandings, for example, may be brought to a story about pets, zoo animals, or family relationships. Emphasizing the meaning will enable the child to use what he brings to the story, rather than being hampered by what he doesn't bring.

The teacher needs to evaluate carefully the student's ability to comprehend. This may be done best with informal observation during discussing and questioning. It is suggested that the child's oral language abilities serve as the key reference in this observation and evaluation process. To illustrate, a child may be discussing a story he has read and paraphrasing an event. If the child comprehended and is able to recode the important events into his usual oral language (even though the expressions may be grammatically incorrect and contain inaccurate pronunciation), then comprehension has taken place. This process requires, however, that the teacher has been attuned to the oral language abilities of the child and has established an environment in which the child can express thoughts freely.

The language dependency of the reading act focuses attention on the desirability of teaching reading through many langauge arts and concept development activities. The use of concrete and audio-visual experiences, for example, will facilitate this process. It may be encouraging to note that many concepts have already been developed by the LEP student, so the need for this student is to acquire the labels which describe objects or events.

The most significant factor in the teacher-student relationship is perhaps the teacher's attitude toward the LEP student. This aspect of the classroom environment has received little discussion in spite of the fact that it is considered crucial to the student's progress. When teachers know many effective teaching strategies, the vital link between teaching and learning may well be the sense of selfworth and desire to achieve that has been instilled in the student. It cannot be stressed too strongly that motivation, interest, self-concept, and other aspects of the affective domain must be positively developed and reinforced if the child is to succeed in school.

An understanding of the LEP child and his language abilities will enable the teacher to develop an appreciation of the diversity and differences within the classroom. These differences should be seen as just that and not as deficits. Each child has a language, a culture, and experiences which have combined to help form that unique individual. Knowing and valuing the child, as stressed previously, are prerequisites to making decisions regarding classroom practices, such as, adapting approaches to reading instruction and utilizing specific teaching strategies.

CHAPTER 4

INSTRUCTIONAL ADAPTATIONS

THERE ARE many methods and approaches that can be used to provide reading instruction in the elementary school classroom, but the most widely used is the basal reader approach. While it can be adapted for use with the limited English proficiency (LEP) student, other approaches are more highly recommended. In this chapter, the following approaches and methods are considered: language experience, sight method, oral reading, basal readers, and methods for older learners. In addition, the use of skills management systems with LEP students will be discussed.

Language Experience

The most frequently and consistently recommended approach for introducing reading instruction in English for LEP students, particularly for those students with no previous reading ability, is language experience. Some advantages to the language experience approach are noted by Cheyney (1976). First, if the child's oral language is used, the reading material will reflect the child's syntax and sentence structure, his own command of the language. The comprehension difficulties which may arise from the artificial sentence patterns used in many beginning reading materials will be eliminated. Another comprehension advantage with language experience comes from the vocabulary used. The vocabulary control which is inherent in language experience is that of comprehension, not decoding. The words used in the dictated story are a part of the child's oral language base. And, finally, comprehension is further assured since the story rises from the child's experience background. The child is familiar with the content and it is meaningful.

Harste, Burke & Woodward (1982) emphasized the importance of natural language forms for language learning. They caution, however, that attempts to simplify language for instructional purposes may be counterproductive. This would be the case, for example, when complex, natural language forms are easier to comprehend than more controlled forms. Their research would also support the language experience approach for LEP students.

The advantages of the language experience approach accrue naturally when an individual story is being dictated. When a group story is developed, both vocabulary and syntax may be included which is beyond an individual's grasp of oral English. In this case, the discussion within the group should help the LEP student understand the meaning intended in the story.

A useful adaptation of the langauge experience approach for non-native speakers of English has been suggested by Wiesendanger and Birlem (1979). They recommend extensive oral language activities which may extend over several days before writing the story. For example, after a small group has taken part in an active experience, the teacher discusses it with them and orally develops key vocabulary words and phrases. The vocabulary is practiced orally using sentence patterns modeled by the teacher.

A second activity could follow this and might involve the children drawing about the experience or discussing it at home with other family members. The new vocabulary and words developed in previous stories are then classified in several categories. This activity provides vocabulary review, develops deeper word understandings, and builds concepts.

Another oral langauge activity utilizes a picture relating to the experience which is discussed by the group. Open-ended questions are emphasized to encourage practice with more complete sentence patterns. Only after extensive oral activities are completed is a story dictated, written down, reproduced, read, and reread.

Feeley (1979) described another variation of the language experience approach which was successful with LEP students. This lesson placed more emphasis on reading than on oral language activities, although vocabulary and sentence development did precede the reading. A poem was introduced as a listening activity, then reread with the children joining in on the repetitions, then reread again with most children reciting along with the teacher. A group cooking activity followed with an experience story dictated about it. The follow-up reading emphasized letters, words, and sentences with one beginning sound introduced. As children framed and read each print group, the concepts of letter, word, sound, and sentence were expanded. An open-ended sentence activity followed, using the pattern, I like _____. Complete sentences were written, illustrated, and read by each group member. The lesson ended with copies of the introductory poem distributed and read and the experience story reread once more.

Certainly, the language experience approach with its unifying factors using experiences, oral language, written language, and reading is an appropriate method to use with LEP students. Its unstructured format readily allows teachers to adapt and vary it to fit the specific needs of individual learners or small groups. It is perhaps the easiest method to use with the single LEP pupil who initially requires individual attention for reading instruction. If particular emphasis is placed on the preliminary oral language activities, the language experience method can be used to introduce reading to those students whose base in English is small.

Many teachers may wish to include the langauge experience approach as a part of their reading program rather than use it as the primary instruction program. Because of the flexibility of language experience activities, a program using it in combination with a basal series could be undertaken quite easily. Another plan could be to start reading with the language experience approach and then gradually introduce a basal program. A teacher's aide or volunteer can assist the teacher in many ways. They can record and copy stories, make word cards and follow-up materials, reread with the students, and guide follow-up practice activities. There are many ways to include the language experience method in the total program and teachers should try to find a modification of it that is comfortable for them.

Sight Method

Elementary teachers are aware of the need to develop a large base of immediately recognizable words for fluent reading. Steinberg (1982) suggests that whole word learning may be the appropriate method for beginning LEP students. The memory capacity of young children is noted as an advantage with this method.

Of particular interest is the work of Harste, Burke & Woodward (1982) with very young children using logos, advertisements, and print from the environment. Children are bombarded with print on the TV screen, along the highways, and around the home. These common print forms can provide a natural resource for beginning reading instruction using the sight method.

Steinberg (1980, 1982) described a four-phase program that includes familiarization, word identification, phrase and sentence identification, and text interpretation.

1. **Word Familiarization**. In this phase, children become aware of print and the relationship of spoken and printed words. Word recognition is not developed at this stage. Word cards to identify objects in the room are used. Suggested activities include pointing to the word card and the object, attaching a given card to an object named by the teacher, and matching like cards in pairs.

2. **Word Identification**. A sight vocabulary is developed with nouns and verbs learned first. Only meaningful words are selected for instruction. Steinberg (1982) emphasized that reading instruction for LEP students should be based on language that the students can understand. Thus, words from a child's listening vocabulary would be appropriate for this stage. A variety of instructional activities for word identification are offered in the next chapter.

3. **Phrase and Sentence Identification**. This phase is an expansion of simple word identification and similar teaching activities can be used (see Chapter 5). Once again, meaningful phrases and sentences, preferably from the child's own language, should be used. If words that are not in the child's understanding are included, these should be kept to a minimum with the rest of the phrase or sentence made up of words in the student's listening vocabulary. The sentence structures or syntax level to be used is also important. Gonzales (1981) suggested a method to analyze a stu-

dent's speech to determine the syntax level the child has acquired. Such analysis would be appropriate to ensure that the sentence and phrase constructions used are not beyond the child's language development. However, this assessment is a rather time consuming and demanding analysis for the classroom teacher. Perhaps, an easier approach would be to use phrase and sentence constructions directly from the child's speech.

4. **Text Interpretation**. A suggested approach to introduce print stories is for the teacher to read the story to the child first. The teacher should point to the words as they are read and the child should look at the print. The story is discussed as it is read. Then the story is reread, a sentence at a time, with the child repeating each sentence after it is read. The third time through, the child reads with the teacher filling in as needed. Pointing to the words is continued with each rereading. Many easy-to-read beginner books are available and are appropriate to use at this stage, and of course, language experience stories could be included. Poems are another print resource to use.

Oral Reading

A method of reading instruction for LEP students which is popular in New Zealand and the South Pacific was described and evaluated by Elley (1981). In this method, high interest, short stories with natural language and some vocabulary control for repetition are used. The teacher reads the story to the group and then the teacher and children reread the story in unison. The story is discussed and read again. Individual words and phrases are identified and choral reading is emphasized. In this controlled research study, significant results were reported in both reading comprehension and word recognition for the bilingual children using this method.

Other methods which emphasize oral reading could also be used. For example, Schneeberg (1977) used echo reading (the teacher reads a sentence orally and the student repeats it) as a method to introduce books and then had students listen and reread the story using tapes at a listening center. Hoskisson (1977) used a combination of echo reading and oral cloze in a three-step program for beginning readers. In Hoskisson's procedure, the teacher and children first read a story together using the echo reading technique with finger pointing. Later, the teacher reads the story and leaves out selected words for the child to supply. In step three, the child reads and the teacher supplies words when assistance is needed. While the above approaches were not used with LEP children, they do incorporate many of the features used successfully in bilingual research (Elley, 1981; Steinberg, 1982).

Basal Readers

Basal reading programs are still the most widely used approach in the United States; classroom teachers with single LEP students, therefore, may prefer to provide instruction within a basal program. Ching states that basal readers ". . . probably provide the teacher with the most guidance and help . . . " (1976, p. 35). Basal materials do offer some advantages for reading instruction for LEP students. For example, the material's vocabulary control and frequent word repetitions are helpful for the beginning reader. Coady (1980) considers this control of readability in beginning materials to be very important.

Another positive factor is the instructional pattern most teachers use with basal stories, the Directed Reading Activity format. The specific strengths of this lesson design are in the introductory section, the vocabulary work, and guided silent reading with discussion. The oral interaction among other pupils and the teacher during group discussion and activities is also beneficial. Finally, the basal program's skills structure ensures that major skills areas are not overlooked. The flexible structure of the teachers' guides allows the teacher to select appropriate skills for emphasis or to omit skills that may create confusion for the LEP student.

A disadvantage of basals is in the concept load of many stories. While the vocabulary load is carefully monitored, the concepts introduced are not. In a review of studies dating back to the 1930's, Serra (1953) noted the concern of many researchers regarding the concept burden in basal readers. For most students, many of the concepts in the stories are familiar and relate to their experiences. This may not be true, however, for LEP students, and the number of different concepts presented in several stories may cause a problem. For example, in one unit of a first reader (Smith and Wardhaugh, 1975), stories dealt with fish, animals that help other animals, different types of animal homes, and finding a home for a stray kitten. Concepts from water pollution to symbiotic relationships and from a school of fish to an animal pound were presented.

Sentence structure, especially in beginning readers, may also pose problems for pupils with limited English proficiency. The rather artificial style of such passages as "Ginger's mother said, 'Your pet eats cake. Your pet eats apples. Your pet wants carrots. I think your pet must be a pig,'" (Ryckman, 1978, p. 31) is more difficult than the natural sentence patterns which would be used with the language experience approach. Saville and Troike (1971) feel this problem alone makes basal readers inappropriate for use in bilingual programs.

Kachuch (1981) noted the complex sentence structures used in basals and the comprehension difficulties they produced, particularly from their use of relative clauses. If the syntactic patterns make comprehension difficult for native speakers of English, these comprehension problems would be compounded for students with limited proficiency with the language. Gonzales' (1981) method for analyzing levels of syntactic complexity may be useful for evaluating the difficulty of reading textbooks. The procedure is used not only to assess the child's language level, but also the syntax level of the text. When the text uses sentence constructions above the child's level, Gonzales suggests that introductory activities be used to explain the meaning.

Many basal series today include a heavy dose of phonics with an emphasis on vowels that may be especially difficult for non-native English speakers to comprehend. Some sound differentiations and pronunciation patterns may never be mastered by LEP pupils. A synthetic phonics program which relies on sound blending to learn new words may be inappropriate. The degree of emphasis and mastery required in phonics portions of basal systems needs to be adapted to fit the needs of the learners. For example, certain areas of phonics may need to be omitted depending on the differences in pronunciation patterns between English and the child's native langauge. Basal programs which require rigid application of a phonics approach would be difficult to use with many bilingual students.

Although the teachers' guides with basal readers suggest adapations for use with special learners, six major series recently reviewed by the writers did not include any material regarding instruction for non-native English speakers. The individual lesson activities in these six series also lacked any mention of ideas for teachers with LEP students.

However, Au (1979) presented several suggestions for utilizing the basal reader with LEP pupils. These included using the introductory section of the Directed Reading Activity to concentrate on a discussion of experiences which relate to the story's content. For example, with a basal reader story about horses the prereading discussion would center on the children's previous experiences with them. If background experiences are lacking, a picture, filmstrip, or story illustration could be used to focus discussion on the concepts needed for story comprehension. During guided silent reading, the teacher should use open-ended questions to encourage longer oral responses. If the prereading discussion indicated weaknesses in concepts or the oral language base for understanding the story content, students need careful questioning and discussion in order to comprehend as they read the story. This dialogue should lead to greater comprehension and should not be used only to check recall of story details. Such questions as, *"Why did the painter say what he did to the old man?"* rather than, *"What did the painter say to the old man?"* help to pinpoint misconceptions or problems in understanding the language used in the story.

Certainly, vocabulary introduction work should be emphasized before reading basal stories. Bilingual students should receive more instruction on new vocabulary than native English speakers to ensure their understanding and to increase concept development. Since they may require introductory work on more words than are identified in the teacher's guide, a quick perusal of the story is needed to identify additional words or phrases to be discussed prior to reading the story.

If oral reading is included in the basal lesson, another opportunity for strengthening language occurs. Mace-Matluck (1979) suggests that non-native speakers of English be given many opportunities to hear the written form of the language read to them. For example, daily oral reading of basal stories by other members of the group can provide some of this listening exposure to written English. Additionally, group oral reading and teacher modeling of sentences and phrases help students gain fluency of varying sentence patterns which, in turn, aids comprehension. Perhaps, more emphasis on listening than on individual oral reading by the bilingual child would be helpful. When the non-native English speaker does read orally, the pronunciation patterns used should be accepted and never ridiculed.

In summary, several adaptations in basal reader lessons are useful for LEP students. Special attention on developing background concepts and introducing vocabulary in depth are needed before reading. Skillful questioning during silent reading is required to identify and clear up misunderstandings and to increase the degree of comprehension. More emphasis on listening to the language rather than on oral reading may be useful. With such adaptations, classroom teachers may find that LEP students can progress with their classmates in a basal reading program.

Older Learners

Older students with limited English proficiency who are learning to read in English have certain characteristics which should influence the instructional approach used. Students who have attained some measure of literacy in one language bring important strengths to reading instruction in English, for many reading skills are transferable. Other than specific phoneme-grapheme relationships and vocabulary knowledge, most readiness and comprehension skills can be transferred from one language to another (Ada, 1980). For example, with auditory discrimination, the student who has mastered the differentiation of beginning sounds in Spanish understands not only the concept of same and different but also can apply it to sounds in English. In other words, if the student hears the beginning sound difference between *mesa* and *niña*, the beginning sound difference of *mother* and *never* will also be heard.

The idea of transferability of the many comprehension skills is, of course, dependent on the child's oral language base in English. But with sufficient oral language ability in English, a student who can apply context clues in one language will understand both how to use it and the value of such a skill as reading in English is approached.

However, along with these advantages, the older LEP student is likely to experience more interference from the native language while learning to read a second language. The ability to anticipate the language as the reader reconstructs the author's message is limited by the student's English base. Diaz (1982) stated that development of oral English skills is needed before reading instruction. A level of oral English ability at least up to the level of the reading materials is suggested. Again, Gonzales's (1981) method of matching a student's language ability with the difficulty level of the print seems appropriate.

An older student may require an individualized program for beginning reading instruction. Such a program would benefit from some introductory language experience work and the oral reading methods previously suggested. A reading buddy or tapes can be used for echo reading and fluency practice. The individualized reading method that relies on student selection of reading material and teacher-pupil conferences could be used with several adaptations for the LEP student. Although self-selection is a feature of individualized reading, the group of books from which the first selection is made should be carefully considered. Easy books are recommended; they should contain familiar content from areas of interest to the student.

After a book is selected, a list of key vocabulary words could be introduced in a conference prior to reading. Oral language background in English is of higher priority here than development of sight vocabulary. Discussion of major concepts for the key words is important with the student using the words in sentences. If basic oral language background is lacking for the key concepts in the book, then another book should be selected. If helpful, a two-language dictionary could be used or could be created as the student works through the book. A phonics chart might also be developed as a visual reference for beginning consonant sounds. As the student reads between conferences, a teacher's aide, volunteer, or designated buddy can assist by explaning passages or decoding words.

The teacher may need to schedule more frequent conferences with the bilingual student than is usual with an individualized program. Teacher-pupil conferences should include many of the features of the individualized approach. A discussion of the material read, oral reading, comprehension questioning, review or introduction of skill work, checking of assignments, directions for new work, and purposes for future reading are common features of the individual conference. Adaptations for LEP students would place more emphasis on vocabulary and comprehension, and the all-important area of oral language background. Vocabulary introduction similar to that used in a directed reading activity should be continued.

An advantage of the individualized approach for a bilingual student is that it truly is individualized. Diagnosis occurs continually in the conferences and skill work should follow based on personal needs. Students feel at ease and comfortable with individual conferences and quickly build a working relationship with the teacher. For a student in a new country and school, a feeling of security is an important byproduct of teacher-pupil conferences in the individualized reading approach. Perhaps, the greatest danger with this method is the opportunity for the teacher to leave the student too much on his own. A regular schedule for frequent conferences would help to prevent this.

Skills Management Systems

The widespread use of skills management systems in conjunction with almost every major approach to reading instruction, warrants some consideration of them with LEP pupils. These systems usually employ specific behavioral objectives, criterion referenced tests, and reporting methods for test results as assessment and communication techniques. Many states which require accountability for reading instruction have turned to such systems as indicators of reading progress. Skills management systems may be an integral part of a basal reader program, a supplemental program from another publishing source, or a monitoring system developed by a state or district. However, all systems tend to divide the reading act into a series of small and separate skills which are easily measured. In one review of fifteen supplemental systems, the total number of objectives measured ranged from sixty in a grades one to four program to eleven hundred in a kindergarten to twelve program (Stallard, 1977). The mean number of objectives in kindergarten or grade one to six programs examined in this study was two hundred and ninety-three.

The division of the reading act into many separate skills is viewed by critics of skills management systems as a questionable practice (Smith and Johnson, 1980). Other criticisms of skills management systems relate to the question of whether a heirarchy of skills exists in reading (Harris and Smith, 1980) or whether mastery of the skill relates to reading achievement (Johnson and Pearson, 1975). Still another problem with skills management systems used with LEP students is that they often ignore the language relatedness of reading. Johnson and Pearson (1975, p. 758) state that ". . . language systems — the phonology, grammar and lexicon — are interdependent. In essence, language is indivisible. . . " Harris and Smith (1980, p. 418) are concerned that the use of skills management systems. . . "will result in an instructional program that is abstract, unintegrated, and unrelated to reading as a language-based process." Such fears are particularly well founded when working with LEP students.

Nevertheless, teachers who are using the language experience approach or individualized reading may consider a skills management system a useful adjunct to their programs. Many teachers view the lack of a skills structure to be a disadvantage of the language experience and individualized approaches. Fears of students not achieving skills (particularly when such achievement is monitored by the state) or feelings of inadequacy regarding a totally teacher-planned skills program may cause some teachers to avoid the use of language experience or individualized approaches. In such cases, the supplemental use of a skills management system may be helpful.

If skills management systems can be adapted and modified in

operation they will be more appropriate for use with LEP students than they would be without modification. Smith and Johnson (1980) suggest that teachers select the particular subtests which they will use with any group of students while Karlin (1980) recommends that they be used in moderation. If such cautions can be implemented with skills management systems, they may be made more useful with LEP students. Teachers should be able to omit unnecessary or inappropriate tests and be allowed to disregard mastery requirements in certain areas. Those areas that come to mind for omission for LEP students would be those related to phoneme-grapheme correspondences which differ markedly from the native language. For example, the whole area of vowels must be questioned for many LEP children. A rigid application of mastery requirements for a vast number of miniscule reading skills (especially in decoding) would be unfortunate for such students. Of far greater importance is the student's ability to integrate the total reading process and function comfortably in English in the classroom; these factors, unfortunately, are not included in skills management systems.

CHAPTER 5

TEACHING ACTIVITIES

CLASSROOM TEACHERS usually have a stock of instructional activities to use for specific reading skills. With minor changes, many of these can be used with students who have limited English proficiency (LEP). In the following sections are suggestions for teaching activities, games, and teacher-made materials in the areas of contextual analysis, sight vocabulary, phonics, structural analysis, vocabulary, sentence structure, and comprehension.

Contextual Analysis

Using contextual analysis is an important skill for all readers and is particularly crucial for LEP students. When combined with other word recognition strategies, context clues reinforce meaning and ensure that decoding skills are developed as a meaningful process.

A rebus story can be used to introduce this skill in a motivating way. The following rebus story also reinforces the initial sound of M (Figure 1).

There was a little animal. He was a [rebus image]. He lived on top of a [rebus image]. He made friends with a [rebus image]. The monkey had a [rebus image] on his face. The mouse had [rebus image] in his pocket. The [rebus image] bought ice cream to eat. Soon it was night and the [rebus image] came out. They went home.

Figure 1

41

Blachowicz (1977) suggested several variations of the cloze technique as additional methods to introduce context clues. Children become familiar with cloze procedures when teachers provide the opportunity to fill in obvious words when reading aloud. Following such oral activities, the Zip technique could be used as an easy next step for group work. Zip (Figure 2) utilizes a short selection projected from a transparency with certain words covered with masking tape. The entire selection is read silently, then read orally line by line. After the group decides on each covered word, the masking tape is zipped off to reveal the word and the story is continued. A short poem or experience story could be used as in the example.

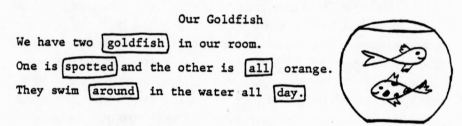

Our Goldfish

We have two [goldfish] in our room.

One is [spotted] and the other is [all] orange.

They swim [around] in the water all [day.]

Figure 2

Synonym cloze, providing a synonym as a clue, is easier for students than the pure cloze format. Another variation of synonym cloze is the maze technique that gives three choices for each blank. The following example (Figure 3) shows both of these procedures.

The cloze technique can also be included for instruction in content area materials. A page of printed cloze material with selected words deleted is distributed to small groups or pairs who work together to determine the words. First, they read the whole page silently to get an overview of the content. Then, the group decides on the most appropriate word to fill each blank. This group activity encourages discussion of synonyms, parts of speech, and grammar. It results in more involvement and enjoyment than would be the case if the activity were completed by the students working individually in a paper and pencil exercise.

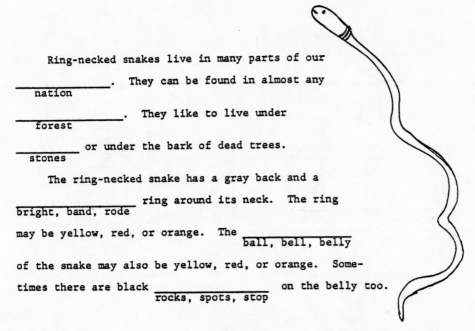

Ring-necked snakes live in many parts of our
_____. They can be found in almost any
  nation

_____. They like to live under
  forest

_____ or under the bark of dead trees.
  stones

The ring-necked snake has a gray back and a
_____ ring around its neck. The ring
bright, band, rode

may be yellow, red, or orange. The _____
                            ball, bell, belly

of the snake may also be yellow, red, or orange. Some-
times there are black _____ on the belly too.
                 rocks, spots, stop

Figure 3

A card game for contextual analysis (Figure 4) requires sentence strips and word cards. The sentence strips can be written on index cards. Each strip contains a sentence with a word deleted. Each player draws four word cards; then the first player turns over the top sentence strip from the pile. If the player has a word card that fits in the sentence, the sentence card and the word card are placed on the table. A player draws another word card to replace the card that was played. If a word card can't be played, the sentence card remains in the center. The next player can play a sentence card that is face up in the center or draw a new one from the pile. Play continues until all the sentence cards are turned up and the winner is the player with the most matches.

File folder activities are one method of organizing student-directed review. In one such activity (Figure 5), the appropriate word is selected to complete each sentence, using context clues for word recognition. A player indicates a choice by pushing a pencil through the hole. A partner tells if the word is correct by noting the circled hole on the back of the file folder.

cat   down

card
pile

was   into

sentence
pile

Mary ____ to
the store

went

"What a game,"
____ Billy.

Figure 4

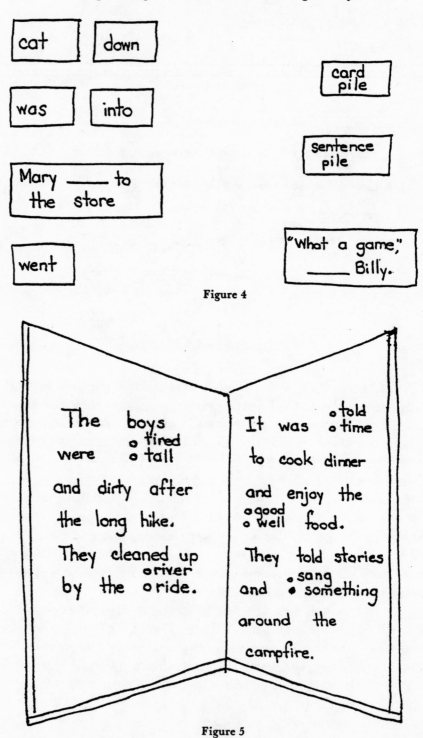

The boys
were ○ tired
      ○ tall
and dirty after
the long hike.
They cleaned up
      ○ river
by the ○ ride.

It was ○ told
       ○ time
to cook dinner
and enjoy the
      ○ good
      ○ well food.
They told stories
and ○ sang
     ● something
around the
campfire.

Figure 5

Students who have trouble using context clues for meaning may benefit from game board activities. Each card contains a sentence with an underlined word defined by the context of the sentence. Players move two spaces on the game board if they can define the underlined word, two more spaces for identifying the type of context clue (definition, comparison, experience, contrast, examples, or mood), and two more spaces if the signal word or phrase is identified. For example, *The stage coach took the safer trail rather than a short but treacherous one*. Treacherous is underlined — it's a contrast type clue and the signal phrase is *rather than*.

Sight Vocabulary

Sight vocabulary activities for LEP students are of greatest value if they emphasize meaning. As long as a meaning clue is included with the target word, almost any of the usual sight vocabulary flash card activities can be used. For example, the addition of a phrase or sentence along with the word to be practiced will help ensure meaning (Figure 6). New words should be presented in context rather than in isolation. When flash card games or activities are used, a picture, phrase, or sentence can be included along with the word on the card.

were

The children ___ playing.

Figure 6

A tape-card reader is a useful tool for sight vocabulary practice. Cards with a picture or a contextual setting for the word are most appropriate. A strong advantage of sight vocabulary practice using a card reader is the self-correcting feature of these machines. In addition, the auditory model heard for each word will help with difficult pronunciation patterns.

If the language experience approach is used, every story will generate word cards to add to the child's sight vocabulary word bank. Again, it is important to present each word in context, using phrases or sentences from the story on the back of the card. These cards can then be used for sentence building, bingo or tic-tac-toe games, writing practice, alphabetizing, classifying, or concentration; in short, they can be used in any game or word card drill. To reinforce meaning, the phrase or sentence should be read when the child identifies the word.

One difficulty with such word card practice activities is the lack of self-correction if they are done individually. It is easy for the child to spend valuable classroom time reading the cards incorrectly and reinforcing errors. Whenever possible, such activities should be developed in game formats in order that other players can check the reading of the word cards. The cards can also be numbered and a taped answer key provided for self-checking of individual activities. Picture word cards for words such as numbers, colors, toys, foods, or animals are another way to decrease the opportunity for practicing mistakes. If the picture and word are on separate cards for matching activities, self-correction can be provided by numbers or symbols on the back or by cutting the cards as interlocking puzzle pieces (Figure 7).

Figure 7

Personal dictionaries can also be developed by the students as yet another way to reinforce sight vocabulary (Feeley, 1983). New words can be pictured and written or used in a sentence or a phrase for later reference in writing activities.

To introduce preprimer vocabulary, Past, Past and Guzman (1980) suggested a useful technique. Following development of language experience stories, nouns are introduced with pictures and then verbs are added. Word cards are used to develop the simple sentences of the preprimers. After much practice building, reading, and rereading the word card sentences, the books are introduced with the same sentences to be read. Thus, an easy transition from language experience to basal materials is provided in a meaningful way.

Some oral sentence patterning may be useful as the bilingual student gains oral fluency. If a basic sentence pattern is repeated with word substitutions introduced, oral practice can be followed by reading, with the basic sentence printed on the board and word substitutions provided from individual word banks. Using this technique, four strategies have been suggested to strengthen both sentence structure and sight vocabulary (Past, Past and Guzman, 1980). These include:

1) Modeling — the teacher reads the sentence and the children repeat it.
2) Framing — the teacher frames one word in the sentence and asks a child what it is.
3) Substituting — one word is changed within the sentence.
4) Closing — one word is omitted from the sentence. A child reads the sentence without the word and then provides the missing word.

The last strategy builds a useful foundation for developing the use of context clues as a word attack technique later on.

Picture books are an invaluable resource in the development of meaningful sight vocabulary. Moustafa (1980) provided a bibliography of picture books that identifies the language pattern emphasized in each book. The repetition involved in many of these simple stories encourages children to join in and read along or to read after the teacher has provided a model.

A basic game board is an additional tool for practice on high frequency sight vocabulary. More flexibility is possible if the words are provided on cards rather than written on the board itself. A motivating theme such as animals or monsters (Figure 8) can be used to decorate the board. A simple game would require written directions, markers, a die or spinner to determine the number of spaces to be moved, and word cards to be drawn and read by the players. A particularly useful set of word cards would be one containing words frequently used in giving directions in the classroom, such as *circle, underline, match*, or *color*.

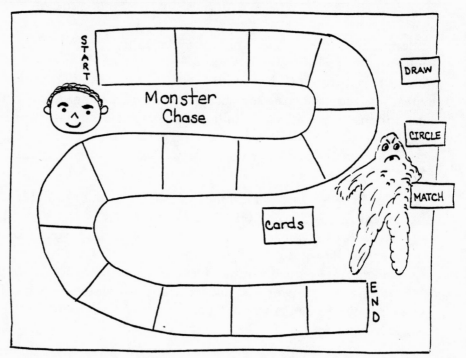

Figure 8

Activities similar to rummy games can emphasize troublesome words from early reading materials. A sentence from a story can be printed on an index card, omitting the word to be emphasized. A word card is also required for the missing word. Sets of twenty to thirty sentences and word cards are needed (some cards of inappropriate words can also be included). In this activity, the sentence cards are dealt out equally to all players with the word cards placed face down in a center pile. Players in turn draw a word card and try to match it with one of their own sentence cards. Matching pairs are placed in front of the player while word cards that cannot be matched are discarded in the center. The players continue to draw from either the word card or discard piles. Being first to match all the sentence cards would qualify a player to go "out" thus being the game winner (Figure 9).

Figure 9

The use of synonyms and antonyms is another way to increase sight vocabulary. Directions for a drawing using antonyms provide variety and opportunity for applying word meaning. For example, in the following activity (Figure 10, Stewart, 1980), students are to do the opposite of the underlined word(s) while following directions:

1. Draw a <u>little</u> tree at the <u>top</u> of your paper.
2. Put a <u>few</u> flowers <u>above</u> the tree.
3. Add a <u>happy</u> child to your picture.

Figure 10

Crossword puzzles and word search puzzles are popular forms for either synonyms or antonyms. If possible, the synonym or antonym for the puzzle should be provided in contextual format to increase meaning as shown in this partial puzzle (Figure 11).

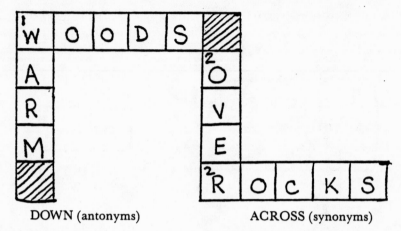

DOWN (antonyms)   ACROSS (synonyms)

1. The water was *cold*.   1. It was dark in the *forest*.
2. The bird flew *under* the nest. 2. They threw the *stones* in the lake.

Figure 11

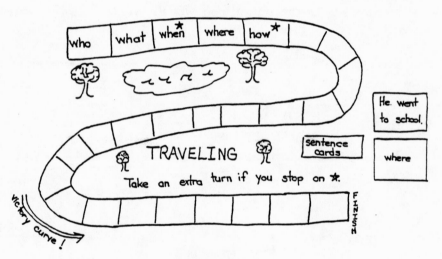

Figure 12

Stewart (1980) suggests Traveling, another sight vocabulary game that reinforces those troublesome question words. Needed are a game board and sentence cards as illustrated above (Figure 12). Each sentence contains an underlined word that would answer a who, what, where, when, or how question. The players in turn draw a card, silently read it, and transform the statement into a question beginning with the appropriate question word. The question is then orally asked. The correct question word is on the back of the card. If the response is correct, the player moves to the next box containing that question word. This game provides practice with question formation while reinforcing basic sight vocabulary.

Students learning to read in their second language especially need an emphasis on sight vocabulary. By including context with sight vocabulary practice activities, the classroom teacher can utilize many familiar techniques to help students develop skills in word recognition and the meaningful interpretation of text.

Phonics

Development of skills in phonics by students whose native language is not English is a far more difficult task than building sight vocabulary. The following guidelines for phonics work are suggested for the classroom teacher:

1. Emphasize beginning consonants, digraphs, and blends, concentrating initially on those that are the same or similar in both languages.
2. Use context clues and phonics in combination by presenting phonics activities in sentences whenever possible.
3. Increase auditory discrimination work, progressing to the more difficult contrasts that do not occur in the native language.
4. Avoid synthetic phonics materials or programs with a heavy phonics emphasis (especially vowel work).
5. Accept the child's oral reading when mispronunciations are language related.
6. Emphasize the concept that sounds are spelled many different ways in English. Since many languages are quite regular in phoneme-grapheme relationships, this concept many be particularly confusing for the student who is literate in another language.

Auditory discrimination is particularly important for bilingual students. Many phoneme differences in English are difficult for non-native speakers to hear and many words with minimal phoneme differences are heard as homonyms. For example a child who does not differentiate /č/ and /š/ will not distinguish between word pairs such as *chop* and *shop*.

Auditory discrimination practice should precede every lesson in phonics; some suggested teaching activities in this area follow. Objects are placed on a tray or table and a child then chooses those beginning with the target phoneme. Naming each object and talking about those that are unfamiliar will help also to expand the child's oral vocabulary. A short poem read by the teacher would give the student further practice in listening for the particular initial phoneme. Students could respond in some way when the phoneme is heard. Poetry experiences add oral language models for the children to hear and imitate.

Using simple picture cards, one could show and name picture pairs such as bird and dog, asking students to indicate if they start with sounds that are alike or different. This could be followed with a sorting activity for individual practice, which would require that a student sort all the pictures that start like bird. They would then name each picture card and use it in a sentence for a final review. An important point that can be easily overlooked in auditory discrimination work is that the student must understand the concept of same-different. Words such as like, alike, or unlike can be used accurately only if they are in the child's listening vocabulary.

Saville and Troike (1971) suggest that practice in minimal contrast pairs such as *bat-mat, bat-bet, bat-ban* is an important part of auditory discrimination training. Ladders (Figure 13) is an example of a game technique that can be used for it. Each child needs two ladders drawn on a ditto sheet or made from construction paper. Also needed is a supply of markers to cover each rung or space in the ladder and a picture to identify the phoneme for each ladder. If, for example, the initial phonemes in *chop* and *shop* were to be contrasted, a small picture to illustrate a key word for each phoneme would be placed at the top of each ladder. The teacher would call a word such as *chain* and the students would cover one rung of the *chop* ladder with a marker. If incorrect, the marker must be removed. Play continues until one or several children reach the top of one of their ladders.

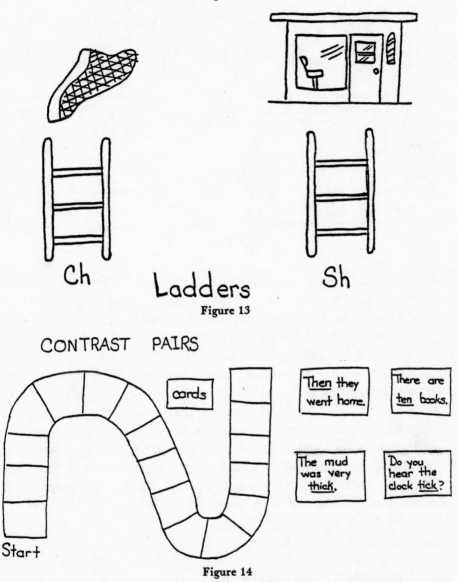

Ch   Ladders   Sh

Figure 13

CONTRAST PAIRS

cards

Then they went home.

There are ten books.

The mud was very thick.

Do you hear the clock tick?

Start

Figure 14

Activities to introduce and reinforce phoneme-grapheme relationships would follow auditory discrimination. A game board format can be used. For example, if the contrast pair *tanks* and *thanks* is emphasized, a stack of cards with words in sentences beginning with either of those sounds is needed, along with the game board (Figure 14). In this activity, each player draws a card, reads the

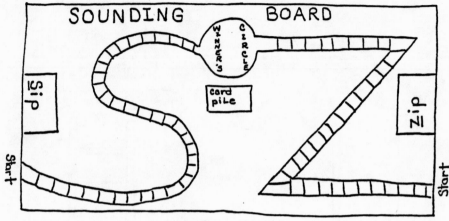

Figure 15

sentence, and identifies the beginning sound of the underlined word. If correct, the player moves as many spaces as there are letters in the word. An answer key can be provided for immediate self-correction. To further assess meaning accuracy, the children could use each word in another sentence.

A variation of this contrast pairs activity can be developed using a game board that has a track for each of the opposing players (Figure 15). An index card labels each track with a word from a minimal pair, such as *zip* and *sip*. A stack of cards with words starting with either sound and a few that start with other sounds is required. Each player selects a sound track, draws a card in turn, reads the word, and identifies the beginning sound. If it is the sound for a particular player's side of the board, the player advances as many spaces as there are letters in the word. The first player to advance to the finish line is the winner.

To include more meaning in such game board activities, one can write the words (underlined) within sentences on the word cards, or require players to use the words in sentences before advancing.

When a new phoneme-grapheme correspondence is being introduced, an appropriate group project could be the construction of a collage (Figure 16). Pictures and objects that start with the new sound can be added daily. A bulletin board or poster board chart can serve as the background. Students need to identify each item and perhaps describe it before adding it to the chart. This will

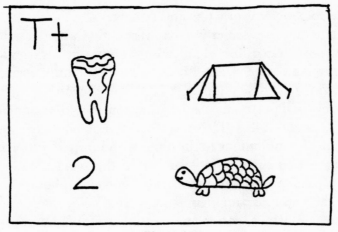

Figure 16

strengthen the oral language base of each student and add to the concept development of the group.

Cassette-ditto materials are useful for follow up skills practice after new sounds are introduced by the teacher. These materials enable the student to hear the sounds and words pronounced and repeated frequently while completing the work sheet.

As stressed earlier in this monograph, context activities are needed if phonics work is to be meaningful. Multiple choice selections in sentence or paragraph formats require students to consider meaning as well as sounds and letters. Sentences such as the following can be put on task cards and used with game boards, tic-tac-toe, or team games for a more motivating practice activity than a ditto sheet.

She stopped to _____ for groceries.
            shop   hop   chop

To summarize, a recommended teaching sequence to follow with a new phonic element would be to introduce it with auditory discrimination activities. The grapheme-phoneme relationship would then be introduced and practiced using contextual materials. Understanding of the relationship can be reinforced by including additional contextual activities along with word card games and cassette-worksheets. Some appropriate activities for minimal-contrast pairs should follow for those sound elements. Activities which emphasize the sound element in context should continue to be used for frequent practice and review.

Instruction in phonics is most productive when activities stress elements in words' initial position. Thorough understanding of phoneme-grapheme relationships will subsequently permit the student to transfer these phonics skills in varied word settings, be they middle or final position. Special attention should be directed also to digraphs and blends. These are often language specific and, as such, may be unfamiliar to the child with limited proficiency in the language of instruction. It is suggested that many of the most frequently used single consonants be covered in phonics instruction before the digraphs and blends are introduced.

More important than the sequential order of phonics skills is the combination of phonics with contextual analysis. Underlying each instructional goal in word recognition strategies is the goal one hopes to reach in the reading program, that is, helping children develop their abilities to have meaningful encounters with text. Stressing the sense, the interpretation of written expressions, by uniting context analysis with the other decoding strategies will encourage students to focus on the desired result of the total reading act while analyzing an occasional smaller unit of its composition.

This emphasis is useful for the teacher to keep in mind in order that mispronunciations and other oral reading behaviors not distract attention from the child's performance in getting meaning. Some children, for example, may never articulate certain English speech sounds. This is especially true for middle and secondary school students who are acquiring English as a second language. The objective of getting meaning, however, depends on gaining concepts portrayed by written text; by stressing context the teacher directs the students' efforts toward this objective.

Structural Analysis

Another area of word attack to consider for students with limited proficiency in English is structural analysis. Many structural analysis activities from the developmental reading program can be used with LEP students. Emphasis on context and meaning is again important. A compound word bingo game might be changed to have the caller read a definition while players cover the appropriate word printed on the board. The statement, *a truck used to put out fires*, would lead to covering the word *firetruck*.

Another game in this area that relies on definitions is Prefix Spin (Figure 17). A spinner with four sections, each marked with a different prefix, is used. A stack of definition cards is needed for each prefix. The player spins, draws a card from that prefix pile, reads the definition, and names the word given. One point is scored for each correct answer. Sample definitions for *re-, pre-,* and *in-* are:

trace again or go over (for retrace)

before dawn (for predawn)

not visible (for invisible)

Figure 17

The Word Tree (Figure 18) reinforces the meaning of Greek and Latin affixes for advanced readers. A drawing of a tree with many horizontal branches is needed as a poster or bulletin board display. A large supply of paper leaves is provided and students place these on the branches in word families. The first leaf on a branch is the prefix and is followed by words that contain the prefix. For exam-

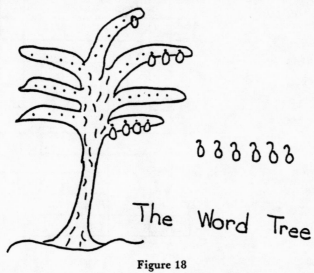

Figure 18

ple, on one branch the prefix is *micro-* with *microphone, microbiology, microscope* following. Other branches have *phone-, multi-* and *cardio-* as prefixes with blank leaves provided for student use. Students are asked to include the words in written sentences and paragraphs as they are added to the tree.

Context can be combined with structural analysis in variations of cloze and maze activities such as these:

1. The statement was un_____ .

2. Please _____ turn the library book today.

   (painting)
3. The (painted) is working in the kitchen.
   (painter)

4. (clean) Paved roads are _____ than dirt roads.

5. I can _____ ten words. On Monday I _____ only five.
   (spell, spelled, spelling, spells)

Sentences can be revised to change meaning by adding or omitting an affix as in these sentences: *He is unlike his brother*, or *The rent was paid*. Such activities can be used with a game board, tic-tac-toe, or a team format.

ACROSS

1. not safe
4. not correct
6. not to like
8. not honest
9. not proper
10. not have sense

DOWN

2. not fiction
3. not true
5. not complete
7. not polite

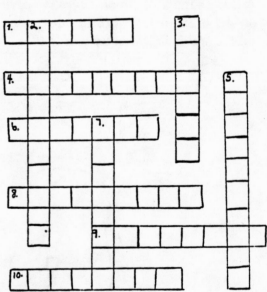

Figure 19

A crossword puzzle (Figure 19) is another technique that can be used to reinforce structural analysis. The illustrated puzzle (Stewart, 1980) emphasizes negative prefixes.

Contractions also cause confusion for bilingual students. A simple word search format (Figure 20) can be combined with context to provide meaningful practice in this area (Stewart, 1980).

```
E  T  O  N  D  L  U  O  H  S
V  T  D  I  D  N  H  T  O  H
A  C  O  U  L  D  O  A  V  E
H  T  O  N  L  L  I  W  L  W
E  R  A  Y  E  H  T  I  L  O
W  H  E  R  E  V  A  H  I  U
X  H  E  I  S  M  A  D  W  L
I  W  O  U  L  D  X  H  I  D
S  I  T  I  H  E  W  I  L  L
L  E  T  U  S  T  O  N  O  D
```

Directions: Find the two words for each underlined contraction in the grid above. Write the words on your paper for each number.

1. He <u>didn't</u> want to go home.
2. I <u>don't</u> have time to do it.
3. <u>Haven't</u> you been there before?
4. <u>He'll</u> play ball every day.
5. Are you sure <u>he's</u> the next hitter?

Figure 20

Vocabulary

Comprehension activities should help non-native speakers of English understand vocabulary and sentence structure as well as the usual basic comprehension skills. Some suggested classroom activities in each of these areas are but a few of the possibilities.

One simple file folder activity to increase vocabulary is called Feed the Dinosaurs (Figure 21). A dinosaur is illustrated on each inside page of the folder, accompanied by a library card pocket to hold the accepted food cards. Each of the two players selects a dinosaur to feed and, in turn, draws a word card from the pile. The words are to be pronounced, defined, and used in a sentence before they are fed to the hungry animal by placing the card in the pocket by the dinosaur. The teacher can provide an answer key, dictionary, or glossary, depending on the ability of the students and difficulty of the word cards.

Figure 21

Figure 22

A bulletin board display featuring the Opposites Owl (Figure 22) can be an on-going vocabulary exercise. Next to a large owl picture, two columns of slots or hooks provide places for word cards to be matched as opposites. A supply of appropriate word cards is needed for students to match. The cards should be changed frequently and students can be encouraged to generate new card sets to match by supplying blank word cards and a nearby dictionary reference.

Opposites can also be emphasized in an Antonym Word Search (Figure 23, Stewart, 1980). In the easiest form of this puzzle, half of each antonym pair is given. The student is to circle and write in its opposite. To make the activity more difficult, both words can be hidden within the search grid with players keeping score of the total number of correct pairs circled and written down within a designated time period. When checking papers of bilingual students, have the words used in sentences if oral English usage is weak or concepts are uncertain. This can be done with a partner in the class.

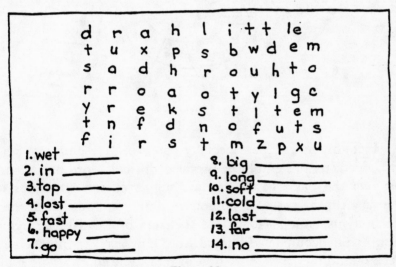

Figure 23

A doggie gameboard (Figure 24) can be used to expand vocabulary via synonyms. A game board decorated with doggie characters and a path to the doghouse is marked off with blank spaces. A word card is placed face up in each space and a synonym is provided in the sentence pile. Each player, in turn, draws a card from the pile, reads the sentence, and locates the synonym card on the gameboard. If correct, the player moves a marker toward the doghouse. The number of spaces to be moved can be determined by a spinner, die, or number written on the word card.

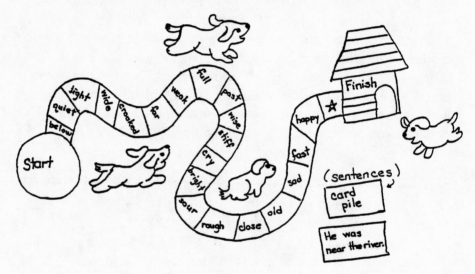

Figure 24

Homonyms can be especially confusing for bilingual students; practice activities emphasizing these difficult word pairs is helpful. Any of the basic game formats suggested for synonyms or antonyms can be used for homonym pairs. In addition to the usual homonyms familiar to native speakers of English, bilingual students will encounter additional word pairs as homonyms due to the lack of auditory differentiation of many sound differences in English. For this reason, the teacher may want to develop separate sets of word pair cards for individual use by particular pupils. In order to do this, the teacher would need to pay close attention to the child's speech and auditory discrimination difficulties to determine the undifferentiated phoneme pairs. For example, the child who doesn't differentiate /s/ and /z/ will consider *sip* and *zip* to be homonyms. Nilsen and Nilsen (1973) is a useful source for word lists of sound pairs in many languages.

Flower Power (Figure 25) is a simple game activity that can be made up in a file folder, on a wipe-off card, or as a chalkboard or bulletin board team game. A series of flowers are drawn, one for each player or team. Each player or team member, in turn, draws a card, pronounces the word, spells the homonym, and uses the selected words in sentences. The homonym is then written on a petal of the flower. One point can be scored for each correct step with up to four points possible for each word card (more points for triple homonyms such as *to, too, two*).

Introductory Examples

bear

tail

meet

Advanced Examples

reign

throne

carrel

karat

Figure 25

Analogies might be used as a vocabulary builder for older bilingual students. A wheel with incomplete analogies and clothespins to match could be used as a format (Figure 26). Written on the wheel might be such analogies as: *Pencil is to write as brush is to* _____. The words to fill in the blanks are written on clothespins which are to be attached to the appropriate place on the wheel. Answers can be placed on the back of the wheel or on a separate answer key.

This wheel and clothespins format is useful for other vocabulary activities that require matching, such as synonyms, antonyms, or

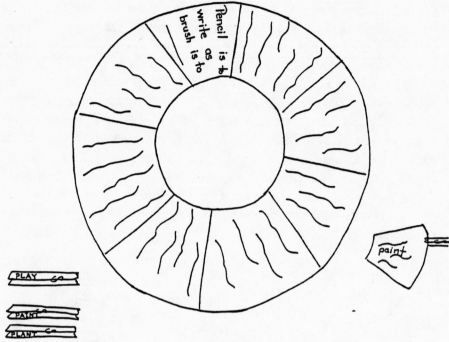

Figure 26

homonyms. Concentration is another game format that can be used successfully with either synonyms, antonyms, or homonyms. Many sets of word pair cards can be developed for this motivating activity to challenge students at various levels of vocabulary ability.

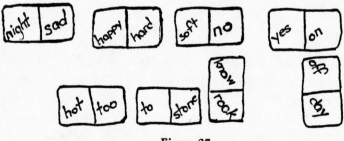

Figure 27

A variation of Dominoes (Figure 27) is a way to combine and review previous vocabulary work with synonyms, antonyms, and homonyms. A large supply of word cards written in domino form is needed for this activity. Five dominoes are dealt to each player with one starting domino card placed face up in the center. Players can join words horizontally or vertically from those in their hand to the starting card by matching any synonyms, antonyms, or homonyms. Each player, in turn, draws five more cards from the deck and plays all suitable cards, scoring one point for each card played. All cards that cannot be played are held by the player for later matches. Players draw five new cards every turn and play as many of the new and old cards as they can on each of their turns. A score sheet is needed for each player and a dictionary is useful as a reference. A good many word cards are necessary for this game to be successful. Workbooks, basal readers, and vocabulary lists are possible sources for the needed words.

Concept building is an important vocabulary tool for LEP students and simple Category Books can be used from the early grades to increase concepts and vocabulary. Booklets made with construction paper covers and blank pages can be filled in with pictures, words or, better yet, words underlined in sentences or phrases (Figure 28). The books can be reread frequently as new pages are continually added.

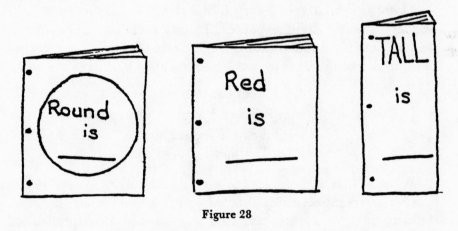

Figure 28

The Question Game, which reinforces meaning of words and phrases, is prepared on a file folder (Figure 29). A large red square is divided into quarters labeled *who, what, where* or *when*. Word and phrase card sets are provided in different colors for each player. The players read the cards and place them in the appropriate section of the red square depending on the question they would answer. Sample cards read: *downtown, later on, a sailor, to the castle,* etc.

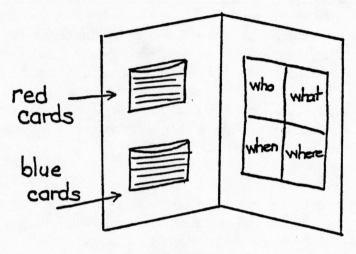

Figure 29

Many informal vocabulary builders send students to the dictionary to verify their responses. In one such activity, a word is printed in two parallel columns as illustrated below. The student is to fill in across the lines to make a new word.

r	d	A word for the first row would have to start
e	a	with *r* and end with *d*, such as *road*. On the
a	e	second row *era* could be used, starting with
d	r	*e* and ending in *a*.

When bilingual students take part in vocabulary activities of this type, teachers must be sure that the words written in are discussed, defined, or used in sentences. This helps to ensure comprehension, increase concept development, and improve English usage.

A classification activity that also functions as a concept builder is called Three by Three (Stewart, 1980). Students work in groups of three to classify words from a list into as many possible groups of three as they can. Each grouping must be written down and the reason for the grouping identified. For example, from the illustrated partial word list given below, *brother, mother*, and *nephew* could be grouped as family members, and *brother, man*, and *policeman* could be grouped as males. A list of from fifty to seventy-five words that can be classified is needed for this activity.

brother	baseball	nephew	plate
magazine	lion	flower	policeman
man	washcloth	dog	bird
petal	mother	fork	sister
frown	teacher	picnic	cup

Sentence Structure

An understanding of sentence structure is crucial to comprehension in English, so activities that reinforce meaning in the sentence unit are important for non-native speakers of the language.

A simple clothesline and cut-outs of clothing can provide motivation for generating sentences (Figure 30). Children use word cards that are clipped with the cut-outs on the line. A group of children can compose sentences with each child adding a word in turn; individuals can develop entire sentences to be hung on the line.

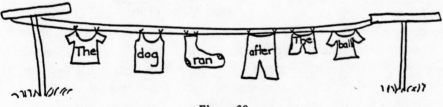

Figure 30

Another way to generate sentences is to place direction cards in a grab bag. Each student selects a card from the grab bag, draws what is stated on the card, and then writes a sentence to describe what is in the picture. A sample card might include the words or phrases *yellow, six, cars, small, by the lake*. These expressions would result in a picture and the sentence, *There are six small yellow cars by the lake.*

To help children understand the meaning of location phrases within sentences, a team activity can be used. A box and supply of objects is placed in front of the group. One member of a team goes to the box and places one of the objects in some position in relation to the box. Another team member then describes the position of the object. Several sentences can be generated by team members as long as they all correctly describe the position of the object in relation to the box. Examples: *The pencil is on the box; the pencil is on top of the box.* One point is given for each correct sentence. A basic sentence should be written on the board with blanks to be filled in and read as each new sentence is formed. Example:

The _____ is _____ the box.

A slot chart can be used in a similar manner to help students formulate and read sentences in English. A chart with four slots or hooks to hold word or phrase cards is prepared. Students need a supply of word and phrase cards that can be combined to form sentences.

Examples

The cat	jumped	over	the table
A girl	walks	to	the door
A large car	is	in	the street

To make the task very easy, the cards and slots can be color coded. More slots or longer phrases can be added later if more complex sentences are desired. Rodrigues and White (1981) and Ching (1976) are excellent sources for sentence patterns and simple dialogues to be practiced orally and then introduced in a reading format.

Another format for developing sentences uses word cards in an envelope. Each child takes one or more envelopes and generates a sentence from the words enclosed. Points can be awarded for the total number of word cards used. In order to keep the materials separated for each envelope, word cards should be color coded or numbered.

The meaning of pronouns within sentences is often difficult for bilingual students to comprehend. A series of activities that increase in difficulty may be helpful. Some written examples with the antecedent and the pronoun to be identified would be a good beginning. The students are asked to circle the antecedent and the pronoun in examples such as these:

1. *Barbara* was upset because *she* forgot to bring the papers home.
2. The children like the *story*. *It* is funny and easy to read.
3. *January* and *February* are winter months. *They* are usually very cold.

Following this, similar sentence activities with the pronoun deleted could be used. In this case, students would write the pronoun in the blank, illustrated in sentence #1 below. Multiple choices of pronouns could be used first if an easier maze format, as shown in sentence #2, is desired.

1. John wanted to play in the game on Saturday, so _____ tried to finish his work on time.
2. The ship was moving slowly across the water. _____ was beautiful to watch.
   It/They/Me

Sentence activities of this type could be mounted in file folders, placed on individual task cards for use with a game board, or used for questions in team games.

A very short story is used for an example of a sentence and phrase comprehension game. First the complete story is read by the children. Phrase and incomplete sentence cards from the story then are matched in a rummy-type game. The phrase cards are dealt out to the players and the incomplete sentence cards are stacked face down in the center. Each of the players, in turn, draws a sentence card and matches it with an appropriate phrase card which is held by that player. If the sentence card cannot be played, the player leaves it in the center and the next player continues the game. A sample sentence is, The squirrel lives _____ , to be completed with the phrase card, in a tree. The winner is the first child to play out all the phrase cards.

Any basic game board (Figure 31) can be used for another game, which reinforces sentence meaning. Students use a die or spinner to determine the number of spaces to be moved after drawing and answering a sentence card. A sentence and a factual or inference question that can be answered from information in the sentence are on the cards. An example at the inference level is: *The boys stood quiet and motionless when they noticed the huge silhouette against the side of their tent. How do you think they felt?*

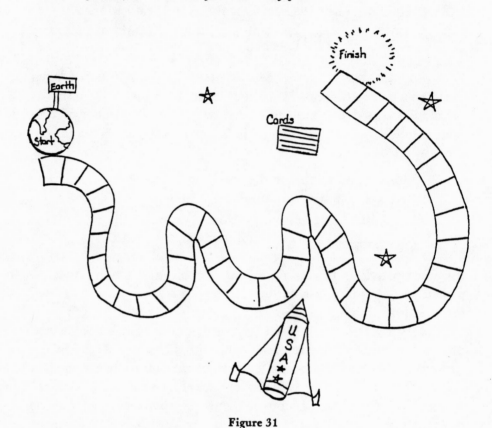

Figure 31

Developing Comprehension

Authorities disagree on the basic comprehension units and whether comprehension is a unified entity or many separate skills. Some separate comprehension skill development, however, seems to help children gain general comprehension of print material. Furthermore, many separate comprehension skills appear in skill lists and/or criterion-referenced or standardized tests. In keeping with their common use in reading programs, some suggestions are offered for activities appropriate for LEP students in the specific comprehension areas of sequence of events, main idea, and noting relationships.

Understanding the sequence of events underlies general comprehension of many reading selections. Oral activities can be used as an introduction to this important skill area. Students can discuss everyday activities and determine the order in which they should occur. If simple two or three item statements are given orally, the students can decide if they are in correct sequence or not. Story pictures can also be placed in sequence to describe the main events of a story. All of these listening or pictorial activities provide a firm basis in working with sequence before the child approaches the skill in printed material.

The Sequence Tree (Figure 32) is an easy-to-make teaching aid to reinforce sentence sequence. A tree with three large leaves and a trunk is cut from construction paper or tag board. These pieces are joined with a brass brad so the leaves can be moved. A sentence is written on each leaf and the student manipulates the leaves to place the message in the right sequence.

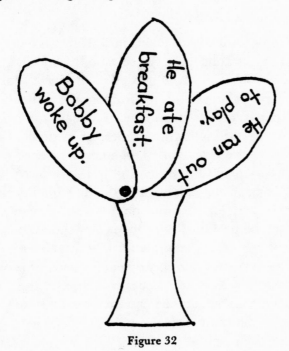

Figure 32

A file folder can be used to develop another manipulative sequence activity (Figure 33) for material of paragraph length or more. A picture is pasted onto a tag board backing sheet and then is cut into strips. The first sentence or portion of the story is written on the back of the top picture strip. The writing continues on the back of each adjacent picture strip so that when the assembled story parts are correctly sequenced, the picture parts are also in the correct order. The separate strips are placed in a file folder in random order. A student reads the cards, places them in sequence in the file folder, closes the folder, and flips it over. When the folder is reopened the picture will show correctly if the story cards were placed in the right sequence.

Figure 33

Another important comprehension skill area is working with the main idea of paragraphs or larger selections. A foundation for this skill is set by classification activities as students learn to group things together by classes and to eliminate those that don't belong. Things That Go Together (Figure 34) is an easy introductory activity that can be used in a learning center or in small groups. Six or more objects that can be classified together are placed in a small paper bag or container. One or two objects are also included that would not belong to the classification. The students should determine the class and identify the objects that do not belong. An answer key can be provided but the teacher should be prepared for students to suggest other classifications, which also may be correct. Bilingual students benefit doubly when this activity is done in small groups. The opportunity to discuss the objects, their characteristics, and possible classifications can increase concepts and classification ability at the same time.

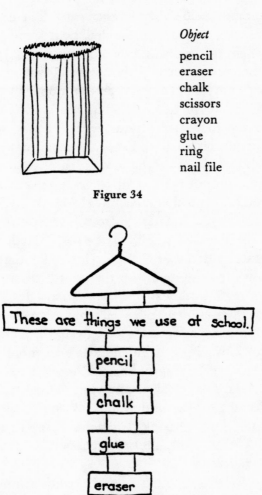

Object

pencil
eraser
chalk
scissors
crayon
glue
ring
nail file

Figure 34

These are things we use at school.

pencil

chalk

glue

eraser

Figure 35

To move from classification into main idea, students could make mobiles using coat hangers, tag board cards, and string (Figure 35). As children determine the classification of a series of words, they can be asked to state the category in a phrase or sentence format rather than just a word. Using the previous example of school supplies, the children may generate a sentence such as, *We work with many materials at school*, or, *These are things we use at school.* To make the mobile, the sentence is written on a large tag board card and suspended horizontally from the hanger. Word cards for the separate objects are strung below the sentence card. The next step is to write the sentence (main idea) on the chalkboard and to generate additional sentences incorporating the objects (details) in a simple paragraph. Students can then generate their own mobiles and follow this later with paragraphs based on the mobiles.

As students begin to understand paragraph formation, topic sentence, main idea, and related details, they will benefit from many opportunities to practice with print materials. Paper and pencil activities to identify the main idea or topic sentence, to find sentences that do not belong, or to arrange sentences into a paragraph format are typical and useful. However, LEP students in particular will benefit at this stage from discussion of such material. Each sentence in a paragraph may be considered, in turn, to determine if it states a detail or the main idea. Another suggestion is to write a main idea statement on the board, discuss each sentence, and determine if it relates to the statement. In this way, students can decide if the statement does tell what the paragraph is all about. Such informal discussion is especially useful when students move from carefully prepared print materials to more general sources. The well structured paragraphs used in practice reading materials are not necessarily typical of all print. Students should move beyond the usual exercise and workbook materials into non-fiction reference material, textbooks, or newspapers to apply their main idea skills. At this point, group discussion to clear up misconceptions once again is crucial.

Helping students understand other relationships in print beyond main idea and supporting details is another aspect of comprehension instruction. Cause and effect and compare and contrast are two more relationships that can be emphasized. A simple and enjoyable format for developing an understanding of cause and effect is Concentration (Figure 36). Eight pairs of cause and effect statements are separately written on numbered cards. Each student turns over and reads aloud any two cards. If they form a cause and effect match, the player keeps the cards. If a match is not made, the cards are turned down again and the next player tries to find a match. An answer key is needed.

Cards and a game board are needed for a suggested compare and contrast activity (Figure 37). Each card contains a pair of

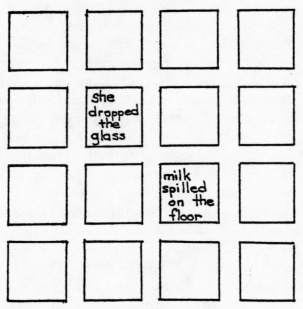

she
dropped
the
glass

milk
spilled
on the
floor

Figure 36

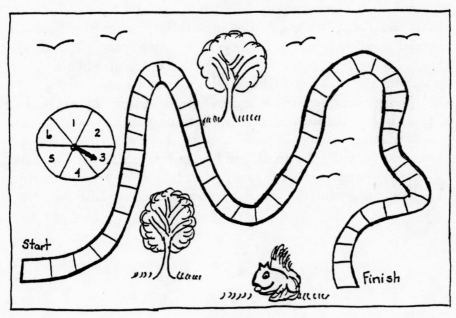

Start

1
2
3
4
5
6

Finish

Figure 37

words that can be compared and contrasted such as rabbit-dog, oak-pine, or happy-angry. Players use a spinner or die to determine whether they compare or contrast the concepts on the cards and the number of spaces they move if correct. If an even number comes up a player tells two things that are alike about the items on the card and two things that are different for an odd number. An answer key can only provide examples or suggestions for this game, so group discussion is often needed to resolve questions raised in the activity. Concept-building is an important extra for non-native English speakers who take part.

If students are to comprehend with ease and fluency, many opportunities to practice reading should be provided in the classroom. Extensive recreational reading is recommended to increase the students' exposure to written language forms (Elley, 1981). A sustained silent reading period is a useful plan to ensure that ample time is available for such practice. Teacher-made skinny books can provide individualized reading materials for LEP students to use for sustained silent reading. Most teachers have access to reading materials that are no longer used in the classroom or have been discarded from the library. These can be taken apart, covered, and stapled to form small individual storybooks. An introductory page, which includes key vocabulary definitions and a page with general comprehension questions at the end, are useful additions. A large supply of non-threatening skinny books on many reading levels is an excellent source of adaptive material that can meet the individual needs of students with limited proficiency in English. Whatever source of materials is used, a daily time period for practice in reading longer contextual material is recommended for LEP students.

CHAPTER 6

CONCLUSION

EVERY CLASSROOM has a variety of students who are un-iquely individual, and all qualities possessed by children contribute to that individuality. These qualities include language competencies that range from strong to minimal within the language of instruction.

In the classroom where English is the language of instruction, the teacher is challenged by the student who has limited English proficiencies. In earlier decades, with less emphasis on meeting individuals' needs, the challenge would have rested on the student, rather than on the teacher. Prior generations of these students provide a source for data on verifying low achievement, high dropout rates, and generally dismal school careers. Statistics on these students will continue to remind educators of the failure of earlier school efforts to provide equal educational opportunities.

Students that lack strong language competencies in the classroom language do not enter the school setting with a linguistic void. They have acquired a language with its systems of significant speech sounds, grammatical structures, and meaningful vocabulary. The effectiveness of classroom instruction, especially in reading, will be enhanced by the teacher's understanding of differences that exist between the student's language and the instructional language.

Special needs of the limited English proficiencies (LEP) child are based on the interrelatedness of the language arts. The level of success reached in reading achievement is greatly dependent upon the abilities that are developed concurrently in listening, speaking, and writing. Furthermore, the development of concepts must underlie all the language arts abilities; only then will students view them as communicative tools for expressing and receiving meaning. Expressiveness is likewise an extension of the child's sense of self-worth and is influenced by the affective climate established and nurtured by the teacher.

The knowledge and attitude of the teacher will subsequently lead to some programmatic changes benefitting the LEP student. These changes may be reflected in a new emphasis on particular word recognition skills and less emphasis on others. Predictable areas of confusion, for example, provide a rationale for excluding specific phonemic elements in the phonics program.

Reading instruction can be adapted to the needs of the LEP student. Language experience, oral reading, sight method, basal reader, and individualized approaches have been found to be useful if the needs of the learner, especially an LEP student, are considered. The value of any approach lies only within the flexibility and effectiveness of its use by a knowledgeable and resourceful teacher. Many suggestions were described previously for adapting and implementing teaching activities and instructional approaches.

The teacher who is able to meet the challenge of the LEP student will have made a significant contribution to society's goal of providing every child with maximum opportunities for academic achievement. Opportunities do not come from courtrooms or administrative offices; they evolve from the efforts of an individual teacher who knows, who cares, who fosters learning.

REFERENCES

Ada, Alma F. "No One Learns to Read Twice," *Aids to Bilingual Communication Report, 1* (January 1980), pp. 2, 4, 7.

Andersson, Theodore and Boyer, Mildred. *Bilingual Schooling in The United States., 1.* Austin, Texas: Southwest Educational Development Laboratory, 1970.

Au, Kathryn Hu-Pei. "Using the Experience-Text Relationship Method with Minority Children," *The Reading Teacher, 32* (March 1979), pp. 677-679.

Blachowicz, Camille L. C. "Cloze Activities for Primary Readers," *The Reading Teacher, 31* (December 1977), pp. 301-302.

Carrillo, Frederico M. *The Development of a Rationale and Model Program to Prepare Teachers for the Bilingual-Bicultural Secondary School Programs.* San Francisco: R and E Research Associates, 1977.

Cheyney, Arnold B. *Teaching Children of Different Cultures in the Classroom: A Language Approach.* 2nd ed. Columbus, Ohio: Charles Merrill, 1976.

Ching, Doris C. *Reading and the Bilingual Child.* Newark, Delaware: International Reading Association, 1976.

Coady, James. "A Psycholinguistic Analysis of Reading in a First Language Compared to Reading in a Second Language." Paper presented at the Twenty-Fifth Annual convention of the International Reading Association. St. Louis, Missouri: May 7, 1980.

Cohen, Andrew D. "The Case for Partial or Total Immersion Education." In *The Bilingual Child: Research and Analysis of Existing Educational Themes.* Edited by Antonio Simoes, Jr. New York: Academic Press, 1976.

Diaz, Joseph O. P. "Factors to Consider When Developing a Reading Program for Puerto Rican Pupils," *The Reading Professor, 8* (1982), pp. 30-33.

"Dragons Slain at Summer Leadership Conference." In *Advocate*, Florida Teaching Profession-National Education Association, *10*, (September, 1983), p. 3.

Elley, Warwick B. "The Role of Reading in Bilingual Contexts," in *Comprehension and Teaching: Research Reviews.* Edited by John T. Guthrie. Newark, Del: International Reading Association, 1981.

Feeley, Joan T. "Help for the Reading Teacher: Dealing with the Limited English Proficient (LEP) Child in the Elementary Classroom," *The Reading Teacher, 36* (March 1983), pp. 650-655.

Feeley, Joan, T. "A Workshop Tried and True: Language Experience for Bilinguals," *The Reading Teacher, 33* (October 1979), pp. 25-27.

"Findings in Current Bilingual Education Research." *Forum.* National Clearinghouse for Bilingual Education *II* (March/April, 1983), pp. 2-3.

Gonzales, Phillip C. "Beginning English Reading for ESL Students," *The Reading Teacher, 35* (November 1981), pp. 154-162.

Harris, Larry A. and Smith, Carl B. *Reading Instruction: Diagnostic Teaching in the Classroom.* 3rd ed. New York: Holt, Rinehart & Winston, 1980.

Harste, Jerome C., Burke, Carolyn L., and Woodward, Virginia A. "Children's Language and World: Initial Encounters with Print," in *Reader Meets Author/Bridging the Gap.* Edited by Judith A. Langer and M. Trika Smith-Burke. Newark, Del: International Reading Association, 1982.

Hoskisson, Kenneth. "Reading Readiness: Three Viewpoints," *Elementary School Journal, 78* (September 1977), pp. 45-52.

Johnson, Dale D. and Pearson, P. David. "Skills Management Systems: A Critique," *The Reading Teacher, 28* (May 1975), pp. 757-764.

Kachuck, Beatrice. "Relative Clauses May Cause Confusion for Young Readers," *The Reading Teacher, 34* (January 1981), pp. 372-377.

Karlin, Robert. *Teaching Elementary Reading: Principles and Strategies.* 3rd ed. New York: Harcourt Brace Jovanovich, 1980.

Mace-Matluck, Betty J. "Order of Acquisition: Same or Different in First- and Second-Language Learning," *The Reading Teacher, 32* (March 1979), pp. 696-703.

Mackey, Ronald, Barkman, Bruce, and Jordon, R. R. *Reading in a Second Language.* Rowley, Massachusetts: Newbury House Publishers, Inc., 1979.

Moustafa, Margaret. "Picture Books for Oral Language Development for Non-English Speaking Children: A Bibliography," *The Reading Teacher, 33* (May 1980), pp. 914-919.

Nilsen, Don L. F. and Nilsen, Alleen Pace. *Pronunciation Contrasts in English.* New York: Regents Publishing Co., 1973.

Past, Kay C., Past, Al and Guzman, Sheila B. "A Bilingual Kindergarten Immersed in Print," *The Reading Teacher, 33* (May 1980), pp. 907-913.

Paulston, Christina Bratt. "Rationales for Bilingual Educational Reforms: A Comparative Assessment" *Comparative Education Review, 22* (October 1978), pp. 402-419.

Robinson, H. Alan. *Reading and Writing Instruction in the United States.* Newark, Delaware: International Reading Association, 1977.

Rodrigues, Raymond J. and White, Robert H. *Mainstreaming the Non-English Speaking Student.* Urbana, IL: ERIC and National Council of Teachers of English, 1981.

Ryckman, John. "Ginger's Upstairs Pet," in *Sunburst*. Edited by William K. Durr, Jean M. LePere, Bess Niehaus and Barbara York. Boston: Houghton Mifflin, 1978.

Saville, Muriel R. and Troike, Rudolph C. *A Handbook of Bilingual Education*. Rev. ed. Washington, D.C.: Teachers of English to Speakers of Other Languages, 1971.

Schneeberg, Helen. "Listening While Reading: A Four Year Study," *The Reading Teacher, 30* (March 1977), pp. 629-635.

Serra, Mary. "The Concept Burden of Instructional Materials," in *Readings on Reading Instruction*. Edited by Albert J. Harris. New York: David McKay, 1963.

Smith, Carl and Wardhaugh, Ronald. *Being Me*. New York: Macmillan, 1975.

Smith, Richard J. and Johnson, Dale D. *Teaching Children to Read*. 2nd ed. Reading, Mass.: Addison-Wesley, 1980.

Stallard, Cathy. "Comparing Objective-Based Reading Programs," *The Journal of Reading, 21* (October 1977), pp. 36-44.

Steinberg, Danny D. "Reading Principles and Teaching," in *Psycholinguistics: Language, Mind, and World*. New York: Longman, 1982.

Steinberg, Danny D. *Teaching Reading to Nursery School Children*. Final Report, U. S. Office of Education, Project No. 5336H90306, Grant No. G007903113. 1980.

Stewart, Adela, ed. "Reading Activities for Bilingual Readers," Tucson, Arizona, 1980. Mimeographed material.

Thonis, Eleanor Wall. *Teaching Reading to Non-English Speakers*. New York: Collier Macmillan International, 1970.

Wiesendanger, Katherine D. and Birlem, Ellen D. "Adapting Langauge Experience to Reading for Bilingual Pupils," *The Reading Teacher, 32* (March 1979), pp. 671-673.

INDEX

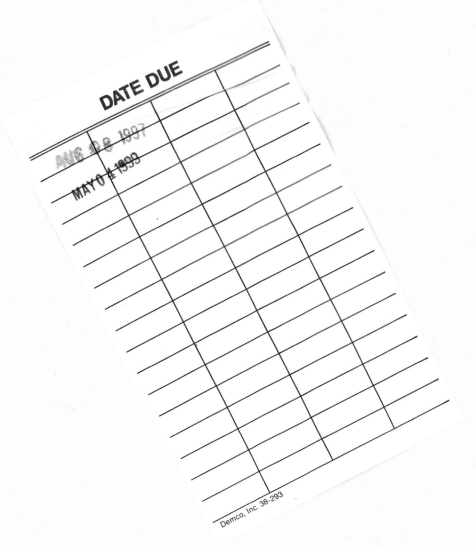

DATE DUE

AUG 29 1997		
MAYO 4 1999		

Demco, Inc. 38-293